FEASTS OF OUR LADY

Fifty talks on feasts of Mary throughout the year with two talks for Mother's Day. Each begins with a story and takes about 8 minutes.

by

Msgr. Arthur Tonne

Imprimatur:
Most Rev. David M. Maloney, S.T.D.
Bishop of Wichita, Kansas

For a complete list of books by
Msgr. Tonne, write to address above.

INTRODUCTION

Behold a feeble tribute to Our Blessed Mother, an effort to acquaint our people with some of her beauties and graces, her privileges and powers.

These talks may be preached on the Sundays preceding the feasts of Mary, in catechism class or study club, on or about the feast.

They may also be adapted for novenas, May devotions, and other Marian exercises.

Your suggestions and prayers are always welcome.

The Author

TABLE OF CONTENTS

TABLE OF CONTENTS (Continued)

OUR LADY OF PROMPT SUCCOR—January 8

"Thou hast done manfully, and thy heart has been strengthened: therefore also the hand of the Lord hath strengthened thee, and therefore thou shalt be blessed forever." Judith 15:11.

An historical film called THE BUCCANEER made its first performance in New Orleans back in 1937. Among the comments one heard expressions like—"Wonderful"—"Gripping"—"Packed with thrills." This talkie was really tense with action, feeling, patriotism and, for the dweller in New Orleans and environs, with the tang of local color.

The movie has to do with the Victory of New Orleans, snatched by the Americans from the British in 1815. It is a screen history of the aid supposedly rendered Jackson's army by the pirate band of Jean Lafitte. The settings are real, the dress, the dance, the deviltry, and the directorial devices are true to the time. The leads and the supporting cast do themselves proud.

Directed by De Mille, the picture is fine, clean entertainment, even though historians find many a flaw in the story. Those in the historical know maintain that Lafitte was far from the field of battle; that he was anything but a polished, soft-spoken gentleman. They bewail the lionizing of this pirate to the dimming of Jackson's glory, while they credit much to the mercilessly accurate marksmanship of the Tennessee and Kentucky backwoodsmen and mountaineers. In proof they dust off the records of the Louisiana Historical Society. Nevertheless, THE BUCCANEER is a colorful fabric of fancy and fact, an entertaining hodgepodge of hokum and history.

But, and I say this with emphasis, this talkie leaves out a most interesting and inspiring phase of the Battle of New Orleans.

Every native of New Orleans knows how the Blessed Virgin helped the Americans win. On the eve of the momentous fray the wives, daughters, sisters and sweethearts of Jackson's valiant little force, gathered at the convent of the devout Ursuline Sisters, and together prayed throughout the night of January 7, 1815.

Their prayers they directed particularly to one who had aided them often before, one whose statue stood above the high altar, Our Lady of Prompt Succor. The next morning at that same altar the Very Reverend William Dubourg, later bishop of New Orleans, offered the sacrifice of the Mass. Meanwhile the Ursuline Superioress had made the vow that, should the Americans be victorious, a Mass of thanksgiving would be sung every year.

Fancy their joy when, at the solemn moment of Communion, a soldier burst into the chapel shouting, "Victory! Victory!"

After Mass Father Dubourg intoned the Te Deum, Holy God We Praise Thy Name. How those anxious women caroled their gratitude! Who but Our Lady had saved their city?

Publicly General Jackson admitted that the God of armies, the Lord of hosts, through His Blessed Mother, had reached out His almighty hand to

2

help. With his staff officers he came in person to thank the nuns for their prayers. Fifteen days later he attended a solemn Mass of thanksgiving in the cathedral.

For over a century the Ursulines have kept their vow to have a Mass celebrated on the anniversary of the battle. Moreover, on the afternoon of every January 8 over 1500 young men and women, organized by the Sodality of Our Lady, march in pilgrimage from Loyola University of the South to the Shrine of Our Lady of Prompt Succor in the Ursuline College Chapel, for services in honor of her who under this title has been elected principal patroness of the city of New Orleans and of the state of Louisiana.

What dramatic possibilities missed by De Mille! The anxious group of women spontaneously joining the sisters in storming heaven throughout the night; the cry, "Victory, Victory" in the quiet of Communion: the battle-weary but grateful Jackson with his tattered men knocking at the convent door to say "Thank You;" these were dramatic realities.

For missing these THE BUCCANEER suffers historically, dramatically. Grant that Lafitte did turn the tide; grant credit to the deadly aim of the American soldiers. Why leave out Our Lady? Why, in the face of history and local tradition, omit to mention Mary's help? It was just another signal example of ready help, of prompt relief, of certain assistance given by Our Lady of Prompt Succor.

As Mary threw her mantle of blue about those who called for her aid in that distant day of distress and danger, so may she cast her protecting garment about us in our present needs. The invading British knocked no more persistently at the gates of New Orleans, than temptation taps daily at the door of our hearts. The enemies of the Catholic Church, who are always the enemies of America, are attacking and invading the city of God. We will do our best to drive them back, but our best will be useless unless we have the assistance of the Lady who has always assisted before.

That assistance we usually need at once, right away. Do you need help —at once, right now? Do you want Mary to help the world situation—right now? Call on her—Our Lady of Prompt Succor. Amen.

ESPOUSALS OF OUR LADY—January 23

"The angel Gabriel was sent from God to a town of Galilee called Nazareth, to a virgin betrothed to a man named Joseph." St. Luke, 1:26.

In the ever interesting and ever inspiring life of St. Joan of Arc we read that an attempt was made in her early days to turn her from her dreams by marrying Joan to a young man of Toul in Lorraine. They went so far as to make a former betrothal. But the saintly maid, who knew from her voices that she had a definite work in the world, would have no part of it.

When she refused to follow up the betrothal with marriage, the future bridegroom had her hailed before the authorities. Obediently she appeared and obediently she answered questions. Her frank and direct answers covered him with confusion. Her common sense, spiced with native wit, confounded and confused the critics of the course she had taken.

In spite of criticism, she persuaded her uncle to take her again to Caudricourt. Again the military authorities, through the captain, bade her to get back to her barn and her cows. She refused to be rejected. For three weeks she remained at the home of a wheelwright by the name of Le Toyer. The maid of Orleans worked as a servant girl in his home. But between domestic duties she found time for prayer.

There is an underground chapel in the town. And in that chapel there is a statue of our Blessed Mother. Before that statue Joan often prayed on her knees for hours.

The determination of the virgin warrior to remain a virgin, to spurn the most enticing offers of marriage, her realization that she had an important work to perform, and her devotion to Mary the Mother of God, are an echo of the trials to which Mary herself was put when the time came for her to be betrothed.

It was the custom for Jewish maidens, when they became of age, to leave the service of the temple and to accept the husband who would be chosen for them. In accordance with this custom, when Mary had reached her fifteenth year, her guardians began to seek a spouse for the beautiful and virtuous daughter of St. Joachim and St. Anne. Orphaned of those parents, Mary had been given into the charge of the priests of the temple. There, together with other maidens, she had led a life of innocence, of retirement, of the exercise of every womanly virtue and task.

When Mary reached the age of fifteen, her guardians decided to unite her in marriage to a man worthy of her. This decision filled Mary with anxiety. To her, virginity was the most perfect, the most holy, the most honorable state a woman could embrace. She had vowed her virginity to God. She preferred to remain in the temple and serve the Lord in a retired and quiet way.

But the guardians of the temple prevailed. And who can doubt that their convincing Mary to accept a spouse was in line with the wishes of Divine Providence? It was the way God chose to protect her from criticism and from offers of marriage from other young men who were attracted by her goodness, but who were not of the high worthiness of the youth who was in the divine plan.

We are all familiar with the legend that tells us how Joseph was chosen from among her many suitors. The evening before the day of the espousals all the young men seeking Mary's hand placed their almond rods in the temple. On the following morning the dried and withered branch of Joseph was discovered fresh and blooming.

This was taken as a clear, miraculous expression of the divine will. And the Blessed Virgin accepted the decision and choice, especially when she realized, as some say, by divine inspiration, that this just man, this lowly carpenter, this virgin husband would always remain so, and would be no closer to her than a protector, a father, a guardian of her chastity.

The espousals were celebrated with simplicity. In the presence of her guardians and some witnesses, Joseph presented her with a small piece of silver or with a gold ring, saying these words: "If thou consent to become my spouse, accept of this pledge."

By accepting the ring Mary became solemnly bound. The scribes drew up the marriage certificate, which was short and to the point. The husband promised to honor his wife, to provide for her support, her clothing, her housing and all her needs.

That very ring with which the espousal of the Blessed Virgin to St. Joseph was performed, is preserved in the Cathedral of Perugia, Italy. It is contained in a richly adorned and precious shrine to the left as you enter the great edifice. Some experts say it is onyx; others that it is of oriental alabaster. The colors it assumes in different lights are amazingly charming to behold.

It was for this chapel where the ring is kept that the famous picture, THE ESPOUSALS OF THE MADONNA, was painted by Perugino. This great work of art is now in the Museum of Caen in France, where it was placed after being stolen by the French government in 1797.

Would that we could hang a copy of that painting in every Catholic heart. Would that we could impress, especially upon the minds of our youth, the scene and spirit of Mary's espousals, the feast we keep on January 23.

Its two outstanding lessons are badly and sadly needed today. The first is the value that Mary put upon virginity, especially virginity dedicated to God, the model of all those virgins who give themselves to the service of the Lord in our religious societies.

The other lesson is the sacredness, the beauty and grace-laden character of modern engagement and marriage. Whatever your walk in life, you can ask Our Lady on the feast of her holy espousals to help you make your choice and to help you carry out that choice. Amen.

PURIFICATION — February 2

"They took him up to Jerusalem to present him to the Lord—as it is written in the Law of the Lord." St. Luke, 2:22.

In the life of St. Dunstan who was born in 910, we read an interesting incident. In fact, this happened even before Dunstan was born. On the feast of the Purification the people went with their usual devotion to the Church of Our Lady. The father and mother of Dunstan were there. All the congregation held lighted candles as they assisted at Solemn Mass. Suddenly, as the Gospel was being read, all the lights in the church went out, including those in the hands of the people.

In the excitement they noticed a candle in the hand of Dunstan's expectant mother. It was lit. From this one light the congregation again relit their candles.

Something like this is expressed in the feast of the Purification, the feast we keep on February 2. St. Luke, 2:22, tells us the story. After Mary had fulfilled all the days of her purification, according to the law, Joseph and Mary carried Jesus to Jerusalem to present Him to the Lord, for it was the law that every first male child should be called holy to the Lord. It was also the law to offer a sacrifice, and they offered a pair of turtle doves. In Jerusalem at that time there was a holy man named Simeon. He was just and devout, waiting for the coming Messias. The Holy Spirit was really in him; that Spirit had told him he would not die until he had seen the Christ, the Lord. He was in the temple at the time and when the parents of Jesus brought in the little Child to do what the law required, this old man took Jesus into his arms, blessed God and said: "Now thou dost dismiss thy servant, O Lord, according to thy word, in peace; Because my eyes have seen thy salvation, which thou hast prepared before the face of all peoples; a light of revelation to the Gentiles, and a glory for thy people Israel." St. Luke, 2:29-32.

Jesus is the Light of the world, as He said Himself: "I am the Light of the world. He that followeth me walketh not in darkness but shall have the light of life." St. John, 8:12.

The Purification is the feast of the Light of the world. We then bless candles, which are symbols of that Light. We place them upon our altars, we carry them in procession, we take them into our homes, to represent Christ, the Light of the world. We do this on February 2 to remind ourselves again that Mary actually carried the Light of the world in the flesh— into the temple. In presenting Jesus, the Light of the world, to the temple and to the hearts of men, Mary showed certain virtues.

I. She was a model of obedience:

    A. This obedience was difficult. Mary had to appear before the priest in the temple as an act of legal purification.

    B. This was blind obedience. She submitted to the letter of the law, although she was not strictly bound to that ordinance.

    C. This was big-hearted obedience. By doing more than her duty demanded, Mary showed her burning love for God.

II. In the Purification Mary showed the deepest humility:

A. **By her virginity.** She preferred not to appear superior to other women, but chose to appear in the eyes of the world, as long as God willed it, less pure than she really was.

B. **By her holiness.** Although she was the purest and holiest of creatures, Mary, on her knees, begged the priest in the temple to pray for her.

C. **By her divine motherhood.** There was nothing external to distinguish Mary from all sinful mothers, even though she was the mother of God. But that was because of the greater delight on the part of God, and because the Almighty had regarded the humility of His handmaid. Therefore, all generations will call her blessed.

III. Mary, in the Purification, is also a model of the most burning love:

A. **She offered up her divine Son.** She offered Jesus, the only delight of her heart, not as a mere ceremony but as a sacrifice in the strictest sense. She offered Him that He might suffer and die and fulfill all that the prophet had foretold about Him.

B. **Out of love Mary brought Jesus back** by the sacrifice of the turtle doves.

C. **Joyfully and tenderly** she carried Him home.

Here we see the three ways in which we can and must offer Jesus, the Light of the world, to the people of the world:

A. By obedience to the laws of Christ's Church we offer Him to the world.

B. By humility, we admit that we are nothing and Christ is all. No matter what our virtues, or our privileges of grace, or our success, even in spiritual matters, we are still nothing and capable of nothing in the sight of the all holy God.

C. By love and by love alone we can win the world. That love is proven by sacrifice. Every act of religion in a sense savors of sacrifice—a giving that is done joyfully, just as Mary made her sacrifice joyfully.

In the story of the Purification we find inspiration for these simple, humble virtues which Mary had and which we also want to have, even in our limited way.

They were the virtues of St. Dunstan and his mother. They are the virtues of all true followers of Jesus and Mary. They are the virtues of all who really show Christ to the world. How the world needs that Light today!

Christ will light up the world if we bring Him to the world, yes, if only to that little world where most of us live. Amen.

7

OUR LADY OF LOURDES—February 11

"Behold, henceforth all generations shall call me blessed." St. Luke, 1:48.

Several years ago Harpers published a book with the title "THE VOYAGE TO LOURDES." It is the work of a famous doctor and scientist, Alexis Carrel. It was edited by his wife and was released six years after the doctor's death.

The story tells of a Dr. Louis Lerrac, which, as you can readily see, spells Carrel backwards. He visited Lourdes in 1903 to see for himself whether cures were really brought about there through prayer to Our Lady. He was particularly interested in one case, that of a Marie Ferrand, who was almost dead of tubercular peritonitis. Dr. Carrel told a friend that if such a case would be cured he would be converted.

Before his astonished eyes, after the water from the shrine had been poured on the stomach of the sick woman, the swelling subsided and her breathing and heart-beat returned to normal. Dr. Carrel had been born a Catholic, but had become a skeptic, one who questions and doubts, especially in matters of religion. He was unable to explain scientifically the remarkable cure which he had witnessed. As a result he returned to the faith of his youth.

In 1935 Dr. Carrel wrote a masterly work entitled "MAN THE UNKNOWN." In its pages he points out that, although we have found out a great deal about man from the standpoint of medicine and surgery, there is still just as much unknown as there is known. He also points out that with regard to the spiritual nature of man we have merely scratched the surface. In this study he defends many of the mystical experiences which take place at Lourdes, France. His experience there had brought about his conversion.

What is Lourdes? Where is Lourdes? Why has it become world famous? The story goes back to February 11, 1858. On that day a little girl fourteen years of age was walking by a rocky cave near her native town. She was looking for pieces of wood to build the fire for her poor parents. She was all alone because her companion had gone on ahead of her.

Suddenly she heard a sound like that of wind. She looked toward the trees, but they were not moving. She looked again, this time to the niche of a rocky grotto. There she saw the figure of a lady, a lady clothed in a white garment with a blue sash. There were golden roses at her feet. Her face was sweet and smiling. In her hand was a rosary.

That little girl was Bernadette Soubirous, who has since been immortalized by being declared a saint, and whose name has been put upon the lips of the world by Franz Werfel's touching account, "THE SONG OF BERNADETTE," and the movie by that name. The rock was the famous Grotto of Lourdes, and the lady she saw was none other than the Blessed Virgin Mother of God.

This was the first vision which Mary granted to Bernadette. The last took place on July 16, 1858, the feast of Our Lady of Mt. Carmel. Our Lady gave the little girl many messages. She told her to drink the water from a spring which suddenly sprang up at the foot of the grotto. She bade the child have the priests erect a church on the spot and then in one of the apparitions our Blessed Lady revealed her name: "I am the Immaculate Conception."

After some delay the bishop appointed a committee to study the appearances. They decided that all were true. A church was erected on the spot. Little Bernadette joined the Sisters of Charity; she never returned to Lourdes. Throughout her life she remained sweet and humble and holy. In 1879 she passed away, and in 1935 Pope Pius XI declared her a saint.

Hundreds of thousands visit that little village each year. And every year hundreds of cures are reported. A group of non-Catholic as well as Catholic doctors and scientists make a thorough investigation of every report.

Hundreds of thousands have returned to their God and their faith because Mary appeared to a little peasant girl in a lonely cavern in the Pyrenees. A group of doctors, including even atheists, have declared that in 1947 and 1948 there were eleven cures which positively and scientifically surpass all the powers of nature.

What are we to think of these miracles? First of all the Catholic Church teaches that it is perfectly reasonable to believe that Almighty God, who created and who sustains the world, may suspend the operation of that physical order where He sees fit. God's Church also teaches that it is entirely in keeping with the wisdom and goodness of God that certain exceptions be made to the rules of nature for the benefit, especially the spiritual benefit, of man. Here are some reasons for such exceptions: God wants to remind men that He really does exist; God wants to remind men of His power, His holiness, His mercy; God sometimes wants to emphasize the authority of some person with a message for mankind.

That was the case at Lourdes. Mary had a message for men, a call to prayer and spiritual life. To back up that message God worked miracles, spiritual as well as physical.

At Lourdes new hope is given to suffering souls. At Lourdes misery and despair are banished. At Lourdes the forces of evil are often broken of their power. At Lourdes many are set on the path to paradise. At Lourdes many realize for the first time Christ's power, Christ's mercy and protection and love.

As we approach the feast of Our Lady of Lourdes, February 11, we will beg her to appear to us with her blessing. We will beg her to help us that one day, like Bernadette, we shall see her face to face, gracious and beautiful and loving, to live forever with her in the company of her divine Son. Amen.

FLIGHT INTO EGYPT—February 17

"Arise, and take the child and his mother, and flee into Egypt, and remain there until I tell thee." St. Matthew, 2:13.

Betty was always an active girl. She was foremost to lend a hand, particularly in parish affairs. In sport and social life, in dramatics, dancing and scouting she was life itself. No wonder her friends expected that a forced inactivity, due to an accident, would be a torture to her. The assistant priest called on her one day and remarked:

"Honestly, I didn't expect to see you so patient, Betty. It must be tough for you to lie here doing nothing."

"It isn't so bad, Father," she smiled. "When I was able to get around, I could almost hear our Lord telling me: 'Betty, do this for me,' or 'Betty, do that;' 'Betty, go here,' 'Betty, go there.' Now that I'm not able to walk, I can almost hear our Lord telling me: 'Betty, stay here and keep still.'"

Her answer seems a far cry, yet it is not so far, to the story of one who heard in the dead of night: "Flee into Egypt," and who heard the other words: "Remain there until I tell thee." Of course, it was not as easy as all that, but at the bottom both young women, Betty today, and Mary centuries ago, both felt and knew that what God wanted was the best.

The second sword that pierced the heart of Mary was wielded by a king named Herod the Great. Great indeed was he, at least in cruelty. When he heard from the Wise Men that they were seeking a Child who was to be a king, he began to fear that those baby hands would snatch the diadem from his head. He ordered that all male children in Bethlehem and the neighborhood two years of age and under should be put to death by the sword.

But the angels of God were swifter than the death angels of men. Hardly had the Wise Men come, adored, and left, when the angel of the Lord appeared to Joseph in his sleep and commanded: "Arise, and take the child and his mother, and flee into Egypt, and remain there until I tell thee. For Herod will seek the child to destroy him."

In other words: "Go there!" "Remain there!"

Mary's heart must have missed a beat, must have throbbed with pain, when Joseph aroused her to the danger. They must go. To leave home, to take the tender Babe on such a rough and cruel journey, to settle among strangers, to make a living in a foreign land, to feel hunted, to face cold, hunger, fatigue, wild beasts and still wilder men—these were the things that sharpened the Second Sword. Our hearts go out to Mary in that pain.

The Bible tells us little more about the flight into Egypt: "So he arose, and took the child and his mother by night, and withdrew into Egypt, and remained there until the death of Herod; that there might be fulfilled what was spoken by the Lord through the prophet, saying, 'Out of Egypt I called my son.'" St. Matthew, 2:14, 15.

How long that sword stayed in Mary's heart we do not know. Some say the exile lasted but a short time. Most believe it lasted seven years—seven years away from home and friends and relatives, seven years toiling for their bread, seven years living in a strange land, seven years fearing that the sword would find Him, seven years of salty tears, seven years as refugees, seven years as truly displaced persons.

From far-off Egypt Mary must have heard the wailing mothers of the Holy Innocents, holding their dead and bloody babes, and crying with Rachel that their children were no more.

She whom we pity in her exile had a heart of pity for those weeping mothers. She has ever had a pitying care for every weeping mother. Particularly is Mary concerned for those who are refugees and displaced persons like her Son and herself. She knows what it means to flee for safety. She knows what it means to be driven from one's home, from friends, from dear ones, to seek haven in a strange land among strange people.

But the victims of war and the displaced victims of godless oppression are not the only objects of her pity. Have we not seen farm families by the hundreds and thousands driven from the land by modern Herods of greed? Do we not read every day of some penniless dweller in the slums being pushed out on the street? Aged parents dispossessed, sometimes by their own ingrate children; hard-working, economical couples losing all to some sharper; even the well-to-do reduced to poverty; the countless thousands of wanderers, young and old, boys and girls, homeless upon the face of the earth; men and families forced by their work and a seemingly heartless system of shifting personnel to move from town to town—like the five-and-ten-cent store manager I know who, just when he is acquainted and established, must pack up the baby's crib and earn the money for its shoes in some distant "Egypt."

With all such seeking sanctuary, economic, political, religious or otherwise, in another land and under another roof, Mary and her Child have a kinship. Those two went through it. They know what it means to fly from injustice—from the sword, from greed, from terror, from all the weapons of modern Herods.

Naturally the Infant and His Mother must feel a special pity for the refugees of war and the families driven from their homes and land by political oppression. As I contemplate and commiserate the plight of Mary and Jesus fleeing in the dead of night from the terror of the sword, I cannot help thinking of the thousands of homeless mothers and fathers and children in war-wrecked Europe and Asia, scurrying and stumbling down the road to find shelter they know not where. As I look at the picture of the flight into Egypt, my newspaper brings me pictures very much like it: here is a Polish madonna with her child fearfully stalking along the tottering walls of a building; there is a French mother and babe hurrying along some high road of France; here is a Belgian woman with her infant crouching beside the wreck of her home.

In them I see Jesus and Mary. And they in turn must know that only Mary and Jesus can help them. The flight into Egypt is being reenacted by modern mothers and infants.

A best-selling novel might paint the soured grapes and with righteous wrath picture the plight of those who must take refuge, of those driven from the family farm, as Jesus and Mary were driven from Bethlehem.

But only those two can do anything about it; only those two can right the wrong that has been done; only those two can console the evicted, the wronged, the refugee, the displaced. Whatever we do in making such flights no longer necessary, whatever we do to harbor the harborless, whatever we do to receive and reestablish the refugee, to locate the displaced, will be a service done to the divine Refugee and His refugee Mother. Amen.

11

"For in him our heart shall rejoice: and in his holy name we have trusted."
Psalm 32:21.

The people of St. Patrick Church, Leicester, England, some years ago were holding a parish dance. As a password to the dance hall they demanded that each one recite the "Hail Mary." The entertainment had been arranged and planned for Catholics only. The test of reciting the "Hail Mary" was required of the dancers to make sure that the rule was obeyed.

It is a far cry from Nazareth where the Angel Gabriel spoke those words for the first time when he cried out, "Hail," to Mary, the chosen Mother of God,—to the door of the dance hall in England where every entrant was required to repeat those blessed words. Yet, just as the "Hail Mary" introduced the youth of St. Patrick parish to an evening of joy and happiness, so the original "Hail Mary" of the angel introduced the world to a new era of joy and blessedness, opened the doors, as it were, to a brighter life and a brighter world, for the Savior of mankind has chosen to be conceived by the Holy Ghost of the Virgin Mary.

In no clearer words can the happy story be told than in the language of St. Luke, 1:26-38:

"In the sixth month the angel Gabriel was sent from God to a town of Galilee called Nazareth, to a virgin bethrothed to a man named Joseph, and the virgin's name was Mary.

"And when the angel had come to her, he said,

'Hail, full of grace, the Lord is with thee.

Blessed art thou among women.'

"When she had seen him she was troubled at his word, and kept pondering what manner of greeting this might be. And the angel said to her,

'Do not be afraid, Mary, for thou hast found grace with God. And behold, thou shalt conceive in thy womb, and shalt bring forth a son; and thou shalt call his name Jesus. He shall be great, and shall be called the Son of the Most High; and the Lord God will give him the throne of David his father, and he shall be king over the house of David forever; and of his kingdom there shall be no end.'

"But Mary said to the angel,

'How shall this happen, since I do not know man?'

"And the angel answered and said to her,

'The Holy Spirit shall come upon thee and the power of the Most High shall overshadow thee; and therefore the Holy One to be born shall be called the Son of God. And behold, Elizabeth, thy kinswoman, also has conceived a son in her old age, and she who was called barren is now in her sixth month; for nothing shall be impossible with God.'

"But Mary said,

'Behold the handmaid of the Lord; be it done to me according to thy word.'

"And the angel departed from her."

What joy in the humble heart of Mary—to be told that she was chosen as the Mother of the long-expected Redeemer. What bliss to know that now the Lord of all was dwelling beneath her heart. She who would have been content to be a servant in the house of the Lord, is told that she is to be the Mother of the Lord.

How sweet the smile that must have played about her lips as she tremblingly but ecstatically accepted the role of Mother of the Redeemer. Poetry, painting, sculpture and music have tried to catch the joy of that moment. But the simple, subdued and beatific smile on the face of Mary expresses it best.

That you might the more devoutly pray the first decade of the Franciscan Crown, "The Immaculate Virgin Mary joyfully conceived Jesus by the Holy Ghost," let your imagination paint a clear and life-like picture of the Annunciation hour.

There is Mary, at prayer in the quiet, simple room of her humble home at Nazareth. She is reading, and prayerfully thinking—thinking and praying about the One who was promised, longing for the day when the Redeemer would come.

Suddenly she realizes that another is present. Looking up, she beholds an angel, whose happy features tell her he is bringing a message of joy. Glorious because he has come fresh from the glory of God, glad because he was chosen for this overwhelming office, the Archangel Gabriel greets her with the words that have echoed round the world—

"Hail, full of grace, the Lord is with thee."

How sweetly, how respectfully, how hopefully, how happily he salutes her. And how humbly, how thoughtfully, she replies. She had hoped to be at least a handmaid or servant in the house of Him who would save all. Here she is asked to be His Mother. If Mary had stammered or swooned with excitement, or if she had set another time for her reply, we would not be surprised. With dignity and joy unspeakable she gives her answer: "Be it done unto me according to thy word."

With that consent Christ becomes present in her, the God whom worlds cannot contain takes up His tabernacle in a tiny house of flesh. For this moment the choirs of heaven had waited; for this hour the faithful, chosen people of God had longed and sighed and prayed. The hour has come.

Realize as best you can what a tremendous honor Mary received, and you will realize partly the bliss she experienced. True Mother of God was she; true Son of hers was the Redeemer. The Holy One now living beneath her heart is the Lord of heaven and earth. Without Him the world always was and always would be dark and dismal. There was no light, there was no joy, there was no promise or hope of happiness—without Him. Mary might have exclaimed:

"Now He is here, right here within me. And He is mine—mine especially —mine to nourish and feed, mine to love and cherish, mine to care for, mine to mother. O God, what joy and bliss is mine!" Amen.

SEVEN SORROWS (Friday after Passion Sunday or September 15)

"And thy own soul a sword shall pierce." St. Luke, 2:35.

Queen Alexandra, the consort of King Edward VII of Great Britain, died in 1925. Two of her three sons had preceded her in death. After her first son had passed away she spent most of her time at Sandringham. It seemed that the only thing which could arouse her interest was some case of sorrow or bereavement that she might lighten.

One morning while out walking the queen met an old woman toiling along the road to Wolferton Station with a heavy load of packages on her back.

"Why are you carrying those things yourself?" asked the queen, "it is too much for you."

"But it cannot be helped, ma'am," was the tearful reply, "my poor boy Jack used to carry them for me; but he is dead, and I must do it myself, or starve."

After expressing a few kindly words of sympathy, the queen passed on. A few days later a trim little donkey cart arrived at the old woman's cottage, a gift of the royal lady who had also lost a son, and who found solace in ministering to the needs of those who were similarly bereft.

There is another Queen Mother who lost a Son, one who was infinitely more precious, infinitely more loving than all the sons of earth. There was another Mother, the Mother of us all, who felt in her loving heart the pain of several swords of sorrow. On the Friday after Passion Sunday Mother Church officially asks us to recall the principal sorrows of Mary, our Sorrowful Mother.

Rightly is our Blessed Mother called the Sorrowful Mother. She is indeed the Mother of Sorrows. She is the Queen of Martyrs. In fact, her whole life was a martyrdom. The sufferings of the poor, for instance, she had to bear all through her life. Mary was poor, as poor, perhaps poorer, than the poorest of us.

A thread of sorrow ran through all her years in that she could see ahead to the time when her only Son, now an Infant, now a little, curly-headed Boy, now an obedient and respectful young Man, would have to die a most painful and disgraceful death.

And oh, her sufferings during the passion of Jesus, her anguish as He carried His cruel cross, her agony as she stood beneath that cross watching Him die. Who could ever measure her grief or count her tears?

It was most fitting that the woman whom God gave us for our heavenly Mother should be a Mother of Sorrows, a woman who had to suffer. As we all know, suffering is the lot of every human being. There is not, nor was there ever, a man, a woman, or a child but had to suffer. No person ever living that had not at least one sword in his heart, at least one sorrow, at least one affliction.

"But so and so has no trials in his life?" How do you know he has none? In judging the sadness or gladness of another life we are much like the tourist who went to visit the pyramids of Egypt. On beholding the great pile of stone and brick from one side, he exclaimed:

"How wonderful!"

The guide, however, beckoning the tourist to follow, took him to the summit from which they could see all four sides of the great work. His wonder and amazement grew, but he was in for still greater surprises when the guide told him to follow into the interior.

Thus it often is with us in our judgment of people. We too often see only one side. The fact remains: Every human being has some sort of sorrow. Is it not consoling then that we children of Mary have for a heavenly Mother one who has borne a many-sworded sorrow? Children of Mary all, we are glad that we have a Mother who suffered too; because only one who has suffered can rightly console, can satisfactorily comfort the sufferings of others.

Yes, everyone has a cross. Bitter indeed are some of our crosses—death of dear ones, sickness, poverty, misunderstanding, difficulties in our home and in our work.

What is your cross? Thank God for it. Ask Mary to show you how to carry it. Our Blessed and Sorrowful Mother, she who sits at the side of her divine Son, with whom she suffered here on earth, Mary is now in heaven waiting to help you, waiting to console you, waiting to be a sympathetic Mother to you.

Next Friday we will recall her principal sorrows. She had many more, but Mother Church centers our attention on the seven swords that pierced her tender heart:

1. The prophecy of Simeon that a sword of sorrow would pierce her heart, was a bitter pain.

2. The flight into Egypt made her experience the sadness of exile.

3. The three-day loss of Jesus made her heart ache.

4. What anguish when she met Jesus on the way of the cross.

5. One would think her heart would break as she stood beneath the cross at Christ's death.

6. Only a mother who holds a dead child in her arms can know anything of Mary's grief as she held Jesus taken down from the cross.

7. Only a mother who puts her child to bed in a grave can understand at all how Mary felt at the burial of Jesus.

Queen Alexandra became a sympathetic and helpful soul through the untimely death of one of her sons. She showed her sympathy to those who grieved and suffered. She had been through it.

Mary, our Sorrowful Queen, reaches out her sympathy and help to everyone who suffers. She, more than any other woman, knew the pang and pain of sorrow. We will go to her and take others to her. Amen.

"For as the sufferings of Christ abound in us, so also through Christ does our comfort abound." II Corinthians, 1:5.

On a busy downtown street in a large mid-western city a street car screeched to a sudden stop. A boy about nine years old, running across the street, was knocked down by the car and was lying under it. The motorman jumped out; people rushed around.

The child was caught in under the machinery in the front of the car. He was badly bruised and scratched, but not critically injured. Nevertheless, he was screaming fearfully:

"Get me out of here. Get me out."

The shock of the accident, the pain and the fear made the boy hysterical. The motorman and the conductor realized that they could not get the boy out without the help of some heavy equipment, which would take about half an hour to arrive from the car barn. Meanwhile the child continued screaming.

A middle-aged woman, rather shabbily dressed, stepped out from the crowd. She knelt down, crawled in under beside the boy, brushed his hair, patted his back and talked to him. Gradually his crying stopped. The boy even tried to smile as this lady spoke to him in soothing words and assured him that in a few moments he would be safely out of his dangerous position. For some 20 or 30 minutes this good woman stayed with the child under the car.

Finally the derrick arrived. The woman gave the lad a parting pat on the head, crawled back out, brushed her dress a bit, and hurried up the street. With her understanding, sympathy and helpful spirit that lady had given comfort and consolation to a terrified and injured little boy.

There is another woman, the woman of all women, who stands ever ready to give consolation to all the children of the world. Her name is Mary, the Mother of God. We call her Our Lady of Consolation, and on April 16 we celebrate the feast of that title.

Every human being at some time or other stands in need of comfort and consolation. This life is filled with distress and depression, with sickness of body and soul, with afflictions of the mind and heart and body. In all these sufferings, in all these terrors, Mary ever stands ready to comfort and console.

1. We pray to her as the comforter of the afflicted. St. Paul tells us in our text that just as we are called to share in many of the sufferings of Christ, so too we can expect the comfort of Christ. In a similar way we suffer the sorrows of Mary, and feel through her that we also will receive comfort. She was a great consolation to her divine Son in His suffering and death.

2. The presence of His mother added to the pains of Jesus, but her being there also made those pains more bearable. St. Ignatius the Martyr says:

"Mary has compassion on the miserable and afflicted, and knowing what it is to suffer, she is ever ready to administer consolation."

3. **Mary consoles the sorrowing by her example.** Although she witnessed and shared Christ's sufferings from the crib to the cross, she never gave way to useless and unrestrained grief. Nobody ever suffered as she did; and nobody was ever as brave and courageous in sorrow as she was. This consoles us.

Solon, the great Greek thinker, one day wished to comfort a friend who had many afflictions. He took him to a lofty hill outside the city of Athens, and, pointing down upon the houses, Solon declared:

"My dear friend, I know and believe that you have some foundation for your dejection, but remember you are not alone. Behold this city and all its houses; how much wretchedness and sorrow prevail in these dwellings! Sorrows to which your tribulations cannot be compared. Be consoled, and reflect that you are not alone, nor the first who suffers."

With these words and this thought Solon, a pagan, made lighter the grief and sadness of his friend.

In a similar way all the afflicted of the world can take their stand on the hill of Calvary, as we point to the Mother of God and the sufferings she bore for Jesus. The sight of our sweet, suffering Mother makes our burden lighter.

4. **From the cross Jesus gave Mary to us as our Mother,** and as a Mother she shows all the tender interest, all the lively sympathy, all the deep devotion, all the compassion and effective charity that are found in the heart of a mother.

5. **Mary also gives actual assistance.** Recall the marriage feast of Cana. Mary noticed the embarrassment of the newly married couple, as the supply of wine ran low. She not only sympathized; she did something. She appealed to her Son, who worked a miracle. We quote St. Bernard:

"Mary has become all to all, and her affectionate heart is open to all, that all may find whatever they need, the slave his liberty, the sick his health, the afflicted comfort, and the sinner pardon."

6. **Often suffering is made bearable by the surety** that there is someone who understands, someone who sympathizes. For a certainty we know that Mary understands and sympathizes and begs her Son to help us in our affliction. She asks Him to give us at least the courage and strength to bear our pain in His spirit.

7. **Through Christian history those who followed and imitated Mary** have been the greatest helpers of the afflicted. Look at the good Sisters in our hospitals, orphan asylums, old folks' homes, yes, and in our leper asylums. In imitation of Mary, Our Lady of Consolation, hundreds of thousands of other ladies of consolation, take care of the afflicted.

Every one of us can imitate Mary as a consoler. Every one of us at some time or other needs consolation. Honor her on April 16, and then Our Lady of Consolation will inspire you to console others and will bring you consolation in your need. Amen.

OUR LADY OF GOOD COUNSEL—April 26

"Hear instruction and be wise, and refuse it not." Proverbs, 8:33.

Francis Suarez, the eminent writer and scholar, was born in Granada in 1548. Though of high blood, he was of low intelligence. The rector at Salamanca refused to admit him to the Jesuit Order. The provincial was advised by his consultors not to admit him. However, this superior of his own accord accepted young Francis into the community on condition that, if he was asked to do so, he would work as a brother.

The youth could make no headway in his studies. Deeply discouraged, he asked permission to become a lay brother. But the superior, edified by such humility and good-will, advised young Francis to try a little longer, and in the meantime to pray fervently to the Mother of Wisdom for help. Suarez had always been devoted to the Blessed Virgin. He did not delay in asking her help; and Mary did not delay in giving her help.

Francis suddenly found that his mind was enlightened and his understanding keen. He readily grasped and absorbed the lectures. He soon became the leader among his fellow students. His name has come down as an eminent theologian and writer.

We recall this incident from the life of a learned man as we approach the Feast of Our Lady of Good Counsel, April 26. It is striking how frequently Sacred Scripture and Mother Church have applied wisdom to Mary. We call her the throne and seat of wisdom because Jesus, eternal Wisdom, dwelt in her womb and had her as a teacher. We are very much in line with the Bible and with Christian history when we go to Mary for good counsel.

1. What does counsel mean? Counsel means advice. It means some recommendation regarding a decision or a course of action or conduct. It also means certain information or instruction, some suggestion or exhortation and admonition. Counsel is more than advice. It is generally given in weightier decisions and on more important occasions.

How is our Blessed Mother the Lady of Good Counsel? Because God gave her unusual knowledge, and also because Jesus gave her particular grace and knowledge during their thirty years together as Mother and Son. As the Mother of Jesus, Mary was His official teacher. An excellent task she performed. The Gospel tells us: "Jesus advanced in wisdom and age and grace before God and man." St. Luke, 2:52.

The mother is the natural teacher of the child. And no doubt God gave us this example of the Holy Family, and especially of Mary teaching Jesus, to inspire and to be a model for all families to come. How it was done we do not know, but why it was done we do know—to give us a model and exemplar.

2. All through history it has been the practice of those devoted to Mary to go to her for intellectual help, to go to her for advice and suggestions in difficult situations.

What Francis Suarez did in the sixteenth century had been done three hundred years before by St. Albert the Great, and then by the Venerable Duns Scotus, the keen Franciscan theologian and thinker. From Our Lady of Good Counsel they received the gift of keen understanding and brilliant intellect.

In the last century another saint, the Cure of Ars, St. John Vianney, who was extremely limited mentally, admitted that it was through the help of Our Lady that he was able to learn enough to be ordained. In a similar way, we today need good counsel. Oh, how the world does need it. Oh, how individuals need it.

3. Think of the various groups who need Our Lady of Good Counsel:

A. What parent will not admit the diffculty in advising and guiding children? From the tiniest tot to the eldest teen-ager, mothers and fathers find it difficult to tell their boys and girls what to do. They find it difficult to tell them how to do it. To parents we recommend Our Lady of Good Counsel. Think over what you would tell your children, and then ask Mary to help you say it, and help them to accept it.

B. Every teacher feels the need of good counsel. To teach means not merely to give new thoughts, new facts. It means guiding, directing, developing the mind and heart and will according to God's plan. Teachers, take Mary as your model and your instructor.

C. Like Suarez, many a student finds it difficult to learn and to remember. No matter what you are studying, Our Lady of Good Counsel will assist you, if you ask her.

D. Our statesmen need this good counsel keenly today. Grant that they are well-intentioned and brilliant, our leaders often know not what path to take to world peace. Why don't we on this feast of Our Lady of Good Counsel, beg our Blessed Mother to guide, inspire and enlighten our leaders and the world's leaders with the best advice?

E. We spend a lot of time talking politics and world affairs, criticizing from the president down to the mayor of the smallest town. Why not devote part of that time to prayer to her who will give good counsel, begging her to guide those in responsible positions?

F. Our Church leaders also need guidance in their weighty problems and heavy responsibilities. Mary will be especially responsive to prayer for her counsel on behalf of those who are the shepherds in her Son's Church.

G. Every single one of us needs good counsel in our personal problems, particularly when we do not know what path to pursue, what course to follow.

Ask her, ask Mary, as did Suarez and many another.

"Our Lady of Good Counsel, pray for us." Amen.

MAY CROWNING

"And when the Prince of the shepherds appears, you will receive the unfading crown of glory." I Peter, 5:4.

It is the troubled year of 1741, in the kingdom of Hungary. We are in a great hall filled with excited men. Their dark faces glow. Their sinewy hands twitch at their swords, ready for action. The question is: Who shall be their ruler?

The crowd sways back and forth. Representatives from the half-savage tribes beyond the Danube are present in their barbaric costumes. Half a dozen kings and dukes are trying to arrange among themselves as to who shall govern Hungary, while the fiery Hungarians themselves will have none of them.

Suddenly a curtain is drawn. All eyes turn to see. There stands a woman in her early twenties, beautiful, with a frank, noble beauty. In her arms she holds her infant son. It is Maria Teresa, wife of Francis, Duke of Tuscany. Through her father, the Emperor Charles VI, she is laying claim to the estates of the Hapsburgs. One of these estates is the Kingdom of Hungary.

She is clad in a brilliant costume with a crown on her head and a sword at her side. She holds her baby aloft and calls upon all present, in the name of her own true knights, begging them to conquer for her inheritance. The enthusiasm is wild. The crowd thrills to the thought:

"This is no mere woman; this is a ruler."

Every man holds his sword on high, as the shout rings out:

"We will die for our king, Maria Teresa."

Their eager energy sweeps all before them. The splendid troops of Hungarian cavalry, the ferocious mountain tribes rise in eagerness. Three years later the husband of Maria Teresa is made emperor. She thus becomes the Empress Queen.

Tonight we are gathered to proclaim and crown another queen, Mary, the Mother of God. There she stands in all her beauty and power. Like those Hungarian soldiers, we too raise our hands and hearts aloft with enthusiastic fervor, crying that we will die for our queen, Mary ever Virgin. In crowning our Blessed Mother tonight we are repeating in our own small way what Almighty God did for Mary when He crowned her as Queen of Heaven and Earth.

1. We know that God crowned Mary with justice. The giving of a crown is usually done in recognition of some deed or of some merit. We crown those who win victories. We crown those who have won success. In every way Mary merited great reward. Her whole life was spent in the service of God. What she said to the angel, "Behold the handmaid of the Lord; be it done to me according to thy word (St. Luke, 1:38), was the theme and object of her entire life—the humble, loving service of the Almighty. Furthermore, Mary merited recognition from God by the fact that freely and out of pure love she consented to conceive and bring forth the Re-

deemer. In this way she gave the Savior to the world. God would recognize this obedience, this cooperation.

The crowning of Mary in heaven proves that God does reward every good deed. Bear that ever in mind. It is expressed for us by the Apostle:

"There is laid up for me a crown of justice, which the Lord, the just Judge, will give to me in that day." II Timothy, 4:8.

2. God crowned Mary with glory. The Almighty presented Mary to the entire court of heaven, adorned as she was with all the gifts of nature and grace. Then the Lord invited all the citizens of heaven to gather around her throne and acclaim her as Queen, Queen of all, Queen of the angels and patriarchs, Queen of prophets and apostles, Queen of martyrs and confessors, Queen of virgins and Queen of all saints. In every one of these groups Mary was a true queen, and when Almighty God crowned her, it was in recognition of this fact.

This scene tonight is a faint echo of that heavenly scene.

3. God crowned Mary with power. King Solomon placed his mother on a throne beside himself, assuring her that he would grant her every request. Christ has placed His Blessed Mother on a throne beside Himself, assuring her of a share in His power. Jesus has power by the fact that He is God; Mary has power by the fact that she is the Mother of God. Only those who never honor Mary make the mistake of thinking that we honor her as a god or a goddess. We honor Mary because God honored her. We crown Mary because God crowned her.

The power with which God crowned her extends to this earth, to those struggling still along the pathway to heaven.

What a consolation, what an encouragement to know that we have a Queen who has received a share in the power of God Himself, power over things of sense, power over things of the spirit.

Tonight as we take part in this solemn crowning, our hearts fly up to the heavenly throne and the heavenly queen. This crown we place on her head here tonight represents the justice and the glory and the power which Almighty God gave to the Mother of His Son. Oh, look at that crown, and let it remind you of the justice of Almighty God. Let it remind you of the glory which God will give to those who serve Him. Let it remind you of the power which God has given to His Mother for your sake.

In the spirit of those Hungarian soldiers who loved their queen, in the spirit of the citizens of heaven and the Christians of all centuries, you and I who love our heavenly Queen, tonight repeat our allegiance to her. To Mary, Queen of heaven and earth, we swear allegiance:

"We want her for Queen. Yes, we will die for our heavenly Queen, Mary, Christ's Blessed Mother." Amen.

MEDIATRIX OF ALL GRACES—May 6

"The mother of Jesus was there." St. John, 2:1.

Recently the ancient and modern mixed when a statue of Our Lady became a first-class passenger on an airplane. Ever since September, 1948, our Blessed Mother, Mediatrix of all Graces, has appeared at a Carmelite Monastery at Lipa in the Philippines. Some time ago a postulant, that is, a young girl who is seeking admission to the Carmelite Order, was privileged to witness several appearances of Our Lady.

This young girl made a statue of Our Lady, Mediatrix of all Graces, and the statue which had the airplane ride is modeled after this original carving. The story is told in a new magazine called "Queen of all Hearts."

The report of the appearances and of the showers of rose petals that fell in Lipa, was brought to Nativity Parish in Litchfield, Connecticut, in 1949. As a result, devotion to Our Lady under this title grew rapidly in the parish, and the pastor arranged to have a replica of the Lipa statue flown to New York in time for the opening of a novena on September 12. However, when it came time to load the crated statue on the plane it was found that it would not pass through the doorway. The crating was removed and the statue rode to the United States in a passenger plane beside Dr. Genaro Vidal, a professor at the University of Santo Tomas in Manila.

As the plane settled down in New York, a crowd from Nativity Parish was there to meet it. They noticed a strong, sweet fragrance described by some as the odor of roses. The statue is now enshrined in Nativity Church, where devotion to Mary under that title, which we honor on May 6, continues to grow.

1. How do we know that Mary is the Mediatrix of all Graces? How is it that she obtains for us every grace? The main reason is this: Mary is the Mother of God, the Mother of Jesus who is true God, the Mother of Christ who is the Author of all grace. Since Mary is the Mother of Christ, who is the Author of all grace, she is naturally the Mother of all Graces.

We must always remember that Mary is the Mother of the entire Christ, and the entire Christ includes you and me. The mystical body of Christ means that you are members of a body of which Christ is the Head. Accordingly, Mary is the Mother, not only of Jesus, but of all those who belong to Jesus. She is the Mother not only of the Head of the mystical body, but she is also the Mother of the members. As a Mother, she trained and cared for Christ. As a Mother, she knew what it meant to perform all those little tasks, to render those thousand and one little attentions which show the true mother. And that same task she performs for us who are members of Christ. Just as she took care of the Infant Jesus, so she takes care of us as infants. Just as she took care of Jesus as a small Boy, so she takes care of us. The same holds for the teens and all through life.

We might put it a different way by saying that we are brothers and sisters of Jesus, because we have a common Father in heaven. As brothers and sisters of Christ Mary takes care of us as her own children.

2. The Bible supports our belief that Mary is the Mediatrix of all Graces.

Recall the marriage feast of Cana. Recall the important words, "The mother of Jesus was there." Yes, Mary was present when Jesus changed the water into wine. She was also there all through the life of Christ. Before He was born Jesus was in the womb of Mary. When St. John was sanctified in the womb of his mother, St. Elizabeth, Mary was there. Mary was in Bethlehem, in Egypt, at Nazareth. She was in the upper room waiting for the Holy Spirit. She was at the foot of the cross, and at the open tomb on that first Easter.

The whole story of Jesus has the golden thread running through it— "The mother of Jesus was there." In a word, Mary shared in the life, the labors, the sufferings, the death and the triumph and glories of Christ. She shared with her Son, and because of this Mary has the blessed task of dispensing the merits which Jesus has gained for us.

3. What the Bible tells us has been believed all through the centuries. The thought that Mary is the Mediatrix of all Graces has been the constant tradition of Christ's Church. The thought is in many early writings. For example, Mary was always called the second Eve, in the sense that through the first Eve and the first Adam man lost grace, while through the second Adam, Christ, and the second Eve, Mary, grace was restored. Listen to St. Germanus of the eighth century:

"No one obtains salvation save through thee, O Most Holy. No one is saved from evil, save through thee, O Most Immaculate. No one is enriched with blessings, save through thee, O Most Chaste. No one receives the gift of grace from God's mercy, save through thee, O Most Highly Honored."

4. This teaching of the ages has been made crystal clear by the popes of the last two hundred years. In letters to the world the Vicar of Christ has pointed out the role of Mary as distributor of God's graces to us all. The divine office of her feast and the Mass for that day, May 6, quotes Scripture and tradition to show that Mary is the source of all grace, the medium of grace to men.

5. Reason offers an argument. God could have given us a Redeemer in some other way than through Mary. But that is the way God chose. Hence, since we receive Christ through Mary, so we receive the graces of Christ through Mary.

We who stand in daily need of God's grace, can do no better than beg for it through Mary. Amen.

QUEEN OF THE APOSTLES (Saturday after the Ascension)

"All these (the Apostles) with one mind continued steadfastly in prayer with the women and Mary, the mother of Jesus, and with his brethren." Acts, 1:14.

Many years ago there lived in Philadelphia a wealthy banker by the name of Francis Anthony Drexel. He was blessed not only with wealth, but also with a pious wife and three virtuous daughters. The parents instilled in their children a deep love of God and of neighbor, encouraging their children to every work of charity.

As a result, one daughter, Elizabeth Drexel, became deeply interested in the poor boys of Philadelphia. Today St. Francis Industrial School at Eddington, Pennsylvania, is a monument to her zeal and generosity. Another daughter, Louisa Drexel, became interested in the negro missions. A third daughter, Katherine Drexel, selected as the object of her charity, work among the first Americans, the Indians.

In his will the father left one tenth of his entire estate, $1,500,000, to charity. About that time Katherine visited the Holy Father. Eloquently she told of her interest in the Indian Missions. The Pope said to her:

"Daughter, why not become a missionary yourself; become a nun and work among them."

Katherine gave up the luxury of their palatial parental home, consulted her confessor, and shortly thereafter became a novice with the Sisters of Mercy in order to begin a new community that was to labor among the children of the forest and the plain. Later her interest extended to the negroes.

Today her spiritual daughters, the Sisters of the Blessed Sacrament, are doing heroic work. Their generosity and zeal know no bounds. Mother Katherine not only supports her own schools but many others. This woman, born to luxury and wealth, sacrificed everything to work for the salvation of souls. She became the mother of a group of modern apostles who carry on the work begun by Christ's chosen twelve.

That work was also done by Mary, the Mother of Jesus. For many reasons we can call our Blessed Mother, Queen of Apostles. On the Saturday after the feast of the Ascension, Mother Church celebrates the feast of Mary, Queen of the Apostles.

1. It is true we cannot call Mary an apostle in the strict sense, in the official sense that she was a priest. In general an apostle means anyone who is sent forth on a mission. It means someone appointed, as was St. Patrick for Ireland, and St. Francis Xavier for the Indies. The twelve whom Christ chose, together with St. Paul, were the official apostles, given grace, given jurisdiction, and endowed with a personal infallibility in regard to faith and morals. Nevertheless, we do speak of Mary as the Queen of the Apostles because she was accepted by them as their queen.

2. The apostles understood better than anyone else the great privileges of Mary. They realized her sanctity; they recognized her virtues; they knew

how she had cooperated in the work of redemption; they knew how Jesus loved her. During the public life of Christ they were closely associated with the Blessed Mother. They were with her through the suffering of our Lord. With Mary they persevered in prayer in the upper room, waiting for the coming of the Holy Spirit. During this long association, even before the death and resurrection of Jesus, the apostles came to know her as their Queen and Mother.

3. The apostles found in the Blessed Virgin, after God, their greatest inspiration. She was still their link with the Lord, after His ascension. Christ had gone to His Father, but He left His Mother with them. We might ask why? Because she was still needed on earth. Our title, Queen of Apostles, tells us why.

4. Mary is also the Mother of Good Counsel. In fact she was the spouse of the Holy Spirit. As such she was the particular adviser of the apostles. That was an outstanding task when you realize the importance of the work of the apostles. They were chosen by Christ Himself, sanctified by Christ, confirmed in grace by our Lord and even told that they would be associated with Him in the judgment. Often the apostles came to Mary for advice and counsel; she told them the path to take, what plan to pursue. Closely associated with Wisdom Herself—our Lord, Mary could share that wisdom with those who were doing the work of her Son.

5. A great measure of the success of the apostles was due to the prayers of the Mother of God. She was Mother of the Infant Christ; she was Mother of the infant Church. God heard her prayer for the conversion of individuals, regions and nations.

6. Mary was an apostle to the apostles in the sense that the wisdom and knowledge God gave her made her a greater teacher than any of the twelve. What might have happened if Mary herself had gone about the world preaching the words of her Son? She would have converted the world. But that was not God's plan. She was to stay in the background and inspire the apostles.

7. Mary is Queen of the Apostles in another sense. The apostles were zealous but they had their defects. They sometimes showed lack of courage, faith, humility and meekness. Mary, on the contrary, had every virtue in perfection, especially those of the true missionary—zeal and the spirit of sacrifice.

We need the example and inspiration of Mary to convert the world. We need her virtues to win the world to her Son. Thank God, our missionaries, our modern apostles, our priests and sisters and brothers, and lay people in the missions, take her for their model. Mother Katherine Drexel is an example of an up-to-date, modern apostle finding her inspiration in Mary, Queen of the Apostles. Amen.

MOTHER'S DAY (First Sermon)

"I am the Mother of fear and of knowledge." Ecclesiasticus, 24:24.

Some years ago the Brooklyn Tablet—one of the best Catholic papers in the country—related the experience of a father who had offered to keep house one day while mother went shopping. This father was an auditor by profession. He had a yen for keeping accounts. Figures were his forte. He could remember them clearly and record them rapidly. He decided to keep a running record of what took place that day. Here are some of the day's totals:

Opened the door for children	106 times
Closed the door for children	106 times
Tied their shoes	16 times
Rescued creeping baby	21 times
Told two-year old George "don't"	94 times
Stopped quarrels	16 times
Spread butter and jelly on bread	11 times
Distributed cookies	28 times
Served glasses of water	15 times
Answered telephone	7 times
Wiped noses	19 times
Answered questions	145 times
Stumped by questions	175 times
Lost temper	47 times
Ran after children (approximately)	4½ miles

The exhausted head of the house had to admit that he might have been too busy to record every time, and that there were incidentals, like picking up toys and taking the scissors away from the baby, which he did in stride without having the second of leisure needed to jot it down.

His list also failed to include the countless other activities of the average mother: washing and ironing and patching and cooking. It lists not the long hours of watching and nursing, the numberless interruptions of sleep to cover the child, to prepare its bottle, see to its feeding and change its essential clothing.

Nor did he record the hours of anxiety when the little one was sick or upset, or when mother was wondering what was going on at school or at play. Neither could he list the wearying worries of mother during the teens of her children.

If you want to get some idea of what your mother did for you, watch the mother with little babies—at home, in church, on the street, on the train or bus. What complete, unselfish, taxing service! Try it. Try to hold twenty pounds of squirming, twisting, bouncing flesh, with two tiny hands that reach out for spectacles, ribbons, hats, and every now and then a fistful of human hair. Try to keep him—or her—from putting the streetcar transfer or your Rosary or the collection envelope into that ever-eager mouth. Try to keep him covered and yet not too warm. Yes, and try to show him off to others without his tumbling over the back of the pew in church or the seat in the street-car. Keep him from crying or yelling when the priest is preaching—if you can.

Once you were a baby like that. Once some mother held you in her arms, fed you and washed you and changed your clothings at least a "dozen" times a day. That mother is your mother. That mother is every mother.

No human auditor or accountant can ever do justice to the ARITHME-TIC OF MOTHERHOOD. It takes a recording angel to add up what mothers do for their children. So, too, no earthly reward can ever compensate for the hours and years, the toils and tears, the heartaches and heartbreaks, a child will cost its mother. Such records are kept only in heaven. Rewards for this work are given only in heaven.

Nevertheless, we make a fervent if feeble attempt once a year to show our appreciation to those who brought us into the world, for what they have done for us. We set aside a day in May to honor them and thank them and do a little problem in the Arithmetic of Motherhood—adding up all their sacrifices, their labors and their pains for us.

Most appropriately we honor mothers in the month which is dedicated to the Mother of us all. Who could ever compute the ARITHMETIC OF HER MOTHERHOOD? Who could ever add up her hours of prayer and loving aspirations, her penances of poverty, her discomforts, her fears and labors and sorrows?

Because she was the Mother of God the Almighty gave Mary every possible beauty and grace. Because she was the Mother of God, we honor Mary on Mother's Day, along with our earthly mothers, who were the first to tell us about our Mother in heaven.

To show our appreciation of the ARITHMETIC OF MOTHERHOOD, we need to add many more tokens of praise, many more expressions of thanks, many more proofs of love to Mary and all mothers. We need to multiply our words of gratitude, our gifts this day and all other days, our smiles of love. We need to divide some of the attention we give less important people and less meaningful things, and give some of that devotion to those who deserve it most—our mothers. We need to subtract a great deal of the forgetfulness, lack of appreciation, and downright ingratitude which we have shown them.

Our heavenly Mother and our earthly mother have done a limitless list of services for us. May we keep adding daily to the little list of things we can do for them. May God reward, as only God can, every service done us by our Mother in heaven and our mother on earth. Amen.

MOTHER'S DAY (Second Sermon)

"Blessed art thou, O daughter, by the Lord the Most High God, above all women upon the earth." Judith, 13:23.

There was a faint and feeble knock at the door of life. Louder and more insistent it grew. Opening the door, the angel of life saw a woman, pale with pain, but with a sparkle of expectant hope in her eye.

"I have come for my child," she said eagerly. "Give it to me quickly. I have come a long way and a hard way. My strength may not last until I return."

"Just a moment," answered the angel slowly. "Your child is here—a beautiful boy. But you must pay for him."

"Pay for him?" echoed the visitor. "My husband and I have very little money. What little we have we will need for the baby."

"It is not money I want," explained the angel. "But I must be paid. I must have some of your health, good woman. I must have a great deal of your time, practically all of it for a few years. You must pay a great deal of your energy, your comfort, much of your peace of mind, and a great portion of your heart."

Without a moment's hesitation the waiting woman handed over all these priceless things. The angel disappeared behind the door of life, to reappear with a wriggling bundle. Eagerly, almost violently the woman clutched him in her feeble arms, thanked the angel, and fearlessly set out for this earth. As the woman turned to leave, the angel gently placed on her head a crown. The lady expressed surprise.

"This is my gift to you," explained the angel of life. "This is the crown of motherhood. This is your reward for the many things you have given up."

The Crown of Motherhood! Who could ever count up its cost? We set aside the second Sunday of every May to place that precious diadem on the head of everyone, living and dead, who has given life to another. Most mothers are too busy to wear that crown every day. Most mothers don't want continual praise and attention. But every mother appreciates at least an annual expression of our love and gratitude. So much the more sincere must it be. So much the more thoughtful, so much the more genuine and heartfelt must Mother's Day be.

Did you ever reckon what small return we make for the price mother paid for her crown? A heap of sweet and sentimental stuff is dished up about this time of year. Some of it is sincere. But carnations, cards, and candy seem so worthless, so weak beside the flesh and blood things mother has given to us. If we could only give her back something of ourselves, something of our time and energy, nay, some of our very blood, some of our very life.

The tremendous difference between what mothers do for their children, and what children do for their mothers was emphasized for me several years ago while traveling by train west out of Kansas City. Because of scarcity of seats a young mother had to hold on her lap her bouncing fifteen-month old boy. Perpetual motion of the baby; perpetual care of the mother. How her arms must have ached; how her limbs must have pained; how her neck must have twitched with stiffness. Every power of mind as well as of body was devoted to that child. Not a moment's rest, not a moment's quiet. Even as he slept there was the tension of tender care. There one saw what mothers do.

Let us now see what some children do. Sitting beside me was another mother, one, I should judge, between fifty-five and sixty years of age. As usual, my Roman collar invited conversation, although she was not a Catholic. In the course of our talk she told me of her family and children. But there was a tearful note in her proud story. One married son living on a farm in Nebraska had not written her a line, nor paid her a visit, nor made a phone call to her in over two years.

The ingrate, the thankless wretch—knowingly or unknowingly such— the ingrate would not give a few moments of time to the one who had given all the moments of many years to him.

No wonder we have Mother's Day.

And no wonder the most loving Son who ever lived thought of His Mother, and provided for her, despite the terrible torture of His dying moments. He was more concerned for her than He was for Himself. His throat was parched, His tongue heavy, His lips bloody, but Jesus knew what the crown of motherhood had cost her. And remembering, He would make some return. He told St. John, He told you and me: "Behold thy mother."

Respect and reverence and thoughtfulness and gratitude toward our mothers is an all-year and an all-life duty. Mother's Day points up that obligation. Mother's Day gives us a reminder and an opportunity to think of what our heavenly and our earthly mother have done for us, and to render some gift or word of thanks.

Yes, "Behold thy mother," your earthly mother and your heavenly Mother, and as we crown them both this May, keep in mind the cost of their crowns. Amen.

OUR LADY OF THE BLESSED SACRAMENT—May 13

"And the Word was made flesh, and dwelt among us." St. John, 1:14.

On the morning of February 23, 1908, Father Leo Heinrichs, a Franciscan priest, was saying Mass in St. Elizabeth Church, Denver, Colorado. Among those who came to the Communion rail was one Guiseppe Alia, member of a secret gang of priest-haters. As soon as father placed the Host on his tongue he spat it out, whipped a revolver from his coat, and fired a bullet through the heart of the priest.

Mortally wounded, Father Leo tried to reach the altar of the Blessed Virgin. He managed to place the ciborium on the altar step. His last effort was to pick up a few Hosts which had fallen.

Two fellow friars were called. One took care of the Sacred Hosts, while the other gave the martyr priest the Last Sacraments. With the names of Jesus and Mary on his lips, between the altar of the Son of God and the altar of His Blessed Mother, the priest passed away. The murderer was hanged.

Only later was it discovered that Father Leo had been living a life of heroic penance and prayer. His canonization is being promoted.

A week before his death he had told the Young Ladies Sodality:

"If I had my choice of a place to die, I would choose to die at the feet of the Blessed Virgin."

His wish was literally fulfilled.

One point stands out in this priest's pious life—the close relationship between devotion to our Lord in the Blessed Sacrament and devotion to Our Lady. In the stories of all the saints these twin devotions go hand in hand. These were the leading loves of the Little Poor Man of Assisi. They characterize all his followers. True Son of St. Francis, Father Leo was devoted to Christ in the Eucharist, and to Mary, His Mother. He knew the meaning and the beauty of the title, OUR LADY OF THE BLESSED SACRAMENT. We celebrate the feast of that title on May 13.

Why do we call Mary that? What is the connection between Mary and the Eucharist? We can reduce the reasons for this title to three:

1. The Body of our Lord, which becomes present on the altar during Mass, which is given to us in Holy Communion, which remains in the tabernacle day and night, is the same Body that was born of the Virgin Mary.

2. Through Mary all God's gifts come to us, especially that greatest Gift— the Eucharist.

3. The life of our Blessed Mother with St. John from the Ascension to the Assumption is the pattern for our life with Christ in the Eucharist.

In every Holy Mass Christ descends upon the altar. In every Holy Mass Christ is wrapped in the "swaddling clothes" of the altar linens. In every Holy Mass Christ is laid in the "manger" of the corporal and chalice. In every Holy Mass Christ speaks to us again through the Gospels. In every

Holy Mass Christ tells us, "Behold thy mother." In every Holy Mass Christ's Body is held up to our gaze and adoration, as Mary held His tiny Body for the three Wise Men to see. In every Holy Mass Christ becomes present in our hearts as He became present in the womb of His Virgin Mother. In every Holy Mass Christ dies again upon the cross. In every Holy Mass we behold the Body of the risen Christ, as Mary beheld Him after His resurrection. In every Holy Mass we receive Christ from the hands of the priest, just as Mary was privileged to receive her Eucharistic Son from the hands of St. John. The same Jesus who was always with her, is the same Jesus who is always with us—Body and Blood, soul and divinity—in the Eucharist.

We call Mary our Lady of the Blessed Sacrament, because through her all God's graces come to us, in particular that most generous gift, our Lord in the Blessed Sacrament. When we call Mary the Mediatrix of all graces we mean—

1. That Mary's influence with the Almighty gets its power from the merits of Jesus Christ, her Son, and not from Mary herself.

2. That only after her Assumption did Mary exercise her powers of intercession in all their helpful fullness.

3. That it is no dogma or article of faith that all graces come through Mary. You need not go through her to be saved. We might put it this way: If one knew of her over-all influence in obtaining graces, and would still deliberately refuse to call upon her, that person would very probably find it extremely difficult to be saved. As St. Irenaeus put it: "As Eve . . . . was through her disobedience the source of death to herself and the entire human race, so Mary . . . . was through her obedience the source of salvation to herself and the whole human race."

Lastly, after the Ascension, Mary lived for years with St. John, who was a priest and an apostle. As such he celebrated Holy Mass and gave her Holy Communion. Mary was thus enabled to live in the Eucharistic Presence of her Son during those years of separation. What a model she is for our devotion to Mass and Communion.

You cannot separate the Mother from the Child. You cannot separate Our Lady from our Lord in the Eucharist. That is why during this month, her month, our May devotions take on a Eucharistic nature. With Our Lady of the Blessed Sacrament we will live through the life of Christ in every Holy Mass; with her we will receive Him lovingly in Holy Communion; with her we will kneel for His blessing in Benediction.

Like Father Leo Heinrichs, the martyr Franciscan priest, we will always honor the Mother along with the Son. We will honor our Eucharistic King and the Lady who stands first in His court. Amen.

"He who is mighty has done great things for me, and holy is his name." St. Luke, 1:49.

That excellent little mission magazine "FAR EAST" brought us some years ago this inspiring story. Tonglu was a village in China. Forty years before the Boxer Rebellion, which took place in 1900, this village was a miserable place, entirely pagan. A squabble between two rival families had given a native priest a chance to enter as peacemaker. He restored peace and he also made many conversions. As a result, when the Boxer Rebellion broke out the settlement had seven hundred Catholics. Many of the faith from native villages fled for protection to Tonglu. The invaders were determined to wipe out these Christians. Ten thousand strong the Boxers attacked. Everyone thought, "Tonglu cannot resist; Tonglu must fall."

But Tonglu did not fall. From June 5 until August 15 fifteen-hundred men, women, and children, all Chinese Catholics, withstood the terrible siege. Finally, the small, poorly equipped garrison drove off the attackers. It was amazing; it was heroic; it was unexplainable.

No, it wasn't. Throughout the seige the Catholics had prayed ceaselessly to our Blessed Mother, Help of Christians. They put her picture in their church. They appealed to her, and through her intercession they were able successfully to defend their town and their homes. To her these Chinese Catholics have given credit also for the prosperity of the people and the growth of the church in Tonglu during the years that followed. On May 24 we celebrate the feast of Mary, Help of Christians.

1. Mary is the help of every individual Christian. When a child is frightened or hurt or in any need it runs to its mother, and mother always helps. When a child cries for help mother rushes to its assistance. That is just what Mary, Help of Christians, does for each one of us. When we are attacked by the enemies of our soul or body, she hurries to our help. We would like to speak particularly of the enemies of our soul:

A. One of the greatest enemies of our soul is the world. By the world we do not mean this earth on which we live. By the world we mean the spirit of the world, a spirit that entirely forgets and neglects God. That is why the bishops of the United States a few years ago published a letter on the greatest enemy of God and His Church in the United States. They called that enemy "Secularism" which means worldliness.

The spirit of the world is not one of faith; it is not one of morals. It is a spirit that condemns or ignores sacred things. It is a spirit that permits and approves immoral entertainment, bad example, divorce, abortion—any of the things which the world would dictate. These practices, of course, are the enemies of the individual soul. Against them Mary is our protection.

B. The second enemy of the soul is the flesh. Ever since the fall of our first parents the spirit has lost its command over the flesh, as St. Paul experienced: "I see another law in my members, warring against the law of my mind and making me prisoner to the law of sin that is in my members.... Unhappy man that I am! Who will deliver me from the body of this death?" Romans, 7:24, 24.

C. The third enemy of the soul is the devil. He was driven out of heaven, because of his pride. Ever since he and his cohorts are trying to drag souls down into hell. The devil is clever. He uses every means to trap us. He makes evil suggestions. He deceives minds and assaults Christian souls. Here again Mary is our help.

2. Mary is not only the help of the individual Christian; she is the sure help of the entire congregation of Christians in the world. That help has been shown so frequently and so powerfully that we are sure the title Help of Christians goes back to the very infancy of the Church. She inspired the early followers of Christ to undergo death for their faith. She helped those harried by heretics. She inspired St. John Damascene to use his pen against the image-breakers. She drove off the Moors. She won many actual battles.

At Lepanto in 1571 she strengthened the soldiers of Christ who went into battle shouting, "Long live Mary." As a result of this victory won through the Mother of God, Pope Pius V, a saint, added to the Litany of Loretto the invocation, Help of Christians, pray for us.

One hundred years later in 1683 the Turks were again driven back through her help. In the middle of the seventeenth century the Irish, fighting for their liberty and freedom, fighting for their very faith, had a picture of Our Lady on their blue standards and about their necks these words, "In God and Our Lady and Rory O'Mare." Their watchword was "Holy Mary." In 1812 Mary saved New Orleans from the British, as our American General Andrew Jackson later testified.

3. Mary is also the special help of the divinely appointed head of God's Church. We have mentioned just a few instances where the Holy Father was helped by our Blessed Mother.

We would like to mention a particular instance. Napoleon took captive the venerable head of the Church, the saintly Pope Pius VII. The emperor had the Pope dragged from one prison to another in the hope of destroying the Church, or making the empire of the Church one of his own. Again Mary's help was in evidence. Christ's vicar was set free.

Like the people of Tonglu and like all lovers of Mary we want to show devotion to her as Help of Christians. We all need her help. Amen.

OUR LADY OF THE HIGHWAY—May 24

"Now in those days Mary arose and went with haste into the hill country, to a town of Juda." St. Luke, 1:39.

In Bismarck, North Dakota, and in Portland, Oregon, there are statues of the same woman. She is an Indian. Both statues were erected in memory of one who helped a group of American explorers to find their way in the great Northwest.

It was the famous Lewis and Clark Expedition. They came upon the home of a trapper named Touissant Charbonneau. They asked him to guide them on their journey west. The trapper answered:

"I'll do it if my wife and son go too."

The soldiers hesitated, because it was unusual, unheard of that a woman and child would go along on an expedition. But their need of a guide forced them to agree.

The Indian woman bore all the hardships without complaint as she blazed a trail over the land which had been familiar to her as a girl, in the years before she had been captured by another tribe. Yet, even to her at times places were puzzling. There were streams that had changed their course, forests which had grown thicker. The path was covered with underbrush. The rations were getting low. Many of the expedition died and only twenty-nine remained after exhaustion and disease had killed the rest. Yet the Indian woman with her baby strapped to her back plunged on. One day, as they stopped to rest, they saw smoke signals. "Indians on the warpath," growled the weary men. Yes, Indians were coming as the white men held their fingers on the triggers of their guns. Suddenly the Indian woman rushed to the open, and in the presence of both groups she fell into the arms of the invading chief. It was her own brother. In a few days the expedition moved on into the Pacific Northwest.

It seems unbelievable that a woman could guide these rough frontiersmen in territory which they did not know, and yet this was done by an Indian woman, whose name, by the way, was Cacagawea, which means Birdwoman.

Like her, Mary, the Mother of God, is also a guide along the paths and highways of the world. In recent years there has developed a devotion to Mary as Our Lady of the Highway. How keenly we need a heavenly guide along the roads where death and serious accident wait at every turn. When we realize that in the last 14 years more people have been killed by automobiles on the highways than have been killed in all the wars of the United States, then we begin to appreciate the dangers of the highway. These are only the physical dangers.

In addition we have the moral, spiritual dangers along the highway to heaven. There is deep need for someone to guide us, someone who will be interested in us, someone who is powerful to protect and to direct. That someone is the Blessed Virgin, Our Lady of the Highway. She knew what it meant to travel. She made seven special journeys.

1. Our Lady journeyed to visit her cousin, Elizabeth: "Mary arose and

went with haste into the hill country, to a town of Juda. And she entered the house of Zachary and saluted Elizabeth...And Mary remained with her about three months and returned to her own house." St. Luke, 1:39 to 56.

During that lengthy and dangerous trip Mary no doubt felt discomfort and experienced the fears of wild animals and robbers.

2. Her second journey was made at the time of Christ's birth. The Bible tells us how she and St. Joseph looked for a place to rest and lodge, but they were turned from every door. St. Luke also describes this: "And Joseph also went from Galilee out of the town of Nazareth into Judea...to register, together with Mary his espoused wife." St. Luke, 2:4.

3. The third journey of our Blessed Mother was made at the Purification, when Mary and Joseph took Jesus to the temple to offer Him to the Lord, and in order to make the customary offering.

4. The fourth journey of Mary was into Egypt, and what an uncomfortable, dreadful trip that was. In the middle of the night an angel told St. Joseph to take Mary and the Child into a strange land to avoid the sword of Herod.

5. St. Luke also tells us about Mary's fifth journey, made when Jesus was twelve years old. Although women and children were not bound to make this particular pilgrimage, Mary and Jesus went with Joseph.

6. Another notable trip was that taken by our Blessed Mother to Cana, where Christ worked His first public miracle at the marriage feast. It meant a sacrifice for Mary to accompany Jesus in honoring this young couple on their wedding day.

7. Mary's seventh journey was that sorrowful one to Calvary. It was a bitter, heart-rending walk with her Son struggling beneath His cruel cross.

Indeed, Mary is a patroness of travelers because she made these journeys. Accordingly, it is very appropriate that we honor her as Our Lady of the Highway. Furthermore, she is interested in every phase of our lives, especially in the end of life. She does not want our lives to end in a sudden, unprepared way as so often happens on the highway.

Devotion to Our Lady of the Highway is growing. As an aid to motorists and travelers in general a new medal has been struck under that title. It was designed by a Franciscan, the Rev. Giles Lawler, of Singac, New Jersey. On the medal we read these words, "LADY OF THE HIGHWAY, BE WITH US ON OUR JOURNEY FOR THY WAYS ARE BEAUTIFUL AND ALL THY PATHS ARE PEACE." On the reverse side is the prayer:

"WE FLY TO THY PATRONAGE, O HOLY MOTHER OF GOD."

Ask Our Lady of the Highway on her feast May 24, to protect you and your loved ones and all other travelers from the material and moral dangers that beset the highways of life. Amen.

QUEEN OF ALL SAINTS—May 31

"I was exalted like a cedar in Libanus, and as a cypress tree on mount Sion."
Ecclesiasticus, 24:17.

Every year for over fourteen centuries the town of Salency, France, has given to some girl the honor of being queen. Once every year some young lady is chosen as a model for the village because of her virtue. Our "queen for a day" programs on the radio are nothing new.

On a particular day the winner, the one chosen, is led to the church by the chief magistrate of the village to hear Mass. In the afternoon she is attended by twelve young girls dressed in white, and escorted by twelve young men of the neighborhood. The procession marches into church where a colorful ceremony is conducted. A crown is placed upon the head of this maiden chosen for her goodness. She is given a silver ring and a blue ribbon, which are souvenirs of King Louis XIII, who once took part in this annual festival.

Suppose that this contest were world-wide and history-wide. Suppose that from all the young women of all times and all places, one was to be chosen who would be a model of virtue. No doubt that choice would rest upon the simple, humble, but virtuous maiden by the name of Mary. She was outstanding in virtue. She was outstanding in goodness. For that reason the Catholic Church honors Mary as the Queen of All Saints on May 31.

This title is of interest to every one of us, because being a saint is our principal task.

1. Every single one of us has been called to a life of holiness, has been called to be a saint. That is the end and purpose for which God created you and me. God has made us that we might know Him, love Him, and serve Him in this world, in order to be happy with Him forever in the world to come. That is why we are on this earth. If we fulfill that purpose we will be saints.

But there was one who in the highest degree fulfilled that purpose, and that was our Blessed Mother. She knew God. She even lived with God day after day in the intimacy of the relationship between Mother and Son. The Almighty poured into her mind and heart the knowledge of heavenly things. By prayer, by spiritual thought Mary came to know God. Furthermore, Mary loved God. She not only loved Him as a human being, as her own Child, as her own Flesh and Blood, but Mary loved her Child as God. She also loved the heavenly Father. Likewise, she loved the Holy Spirit. And Mary served God. Not once did she refuse to do what God had asked of her and what God had inspired her to perform. Her service of God was complete. It was life-long. It was true and sincere. In that sense Mary fulfilled in the highest way the purpose of life—to know, love and serve God. For that reason she is called the Queen of All Saints, the Queen of all those who tried in heroic ways to know, love, and serve God.

2. We call Mary the Queen of All Saints for another reason. Every saint had certain virtues to a high degree. Many of the saints had many virtues, but not one had all the virtues in a high degree. St. Francis of Assisi had

the spirit of poverty, but it was not to be compared to the poverty of spirit of our Blessed Mother. Some saints were known for their purity, but Mary was purity personified. Others were outstanding for their obedience, but Mary was the obedient daughter of God in the highest way. We have saints known for their zeal, their charity, their patience, their generosity. But every one of these virtues Mary had in the highest degree. Hence we call her Queen of All Saints.

3. We give Mary that title in the sense and for the reason that she helped the saints to become holy. In the life of every hero and heroine of God you will find a deep, tender, devotion to the Queen of all holiness. No matter what other devotions the saint may have had he or she was devoted to the Mother of God. Learned and unlearned, they loved our Blessed Mother. Affection for her is a mark of sanctity.

4. We give her this title because Mary obtained for the holy people of all times, the graces which made them pleasing to God, just as at the marriage feast of Cana Mary requested and obtained from her Son a miracle. In dispensing His graces Christ does so at the bequest and request of His Blessed Mother. We can call Mary the Queen of All Saints in the sense that she obtained God's help for them to lead virtuous and pious lives.

5. Mary is the Queen of all those who enjoy the glory of heaven. There are different degrees in that glory. Some saints are greater than others. The Mother of God stands out above them all. Let me quote St. Bonaventure on this point:

"As the Blessed Virgin surpasses all saints in the grace of a virtuous life and merit, so she stands higher than all the elect in the grace of glory and reward."

Yes, Mary is the Queen of those who have led saintly lives. She is the Queen of those who are leading saintly lives, and she is the Queen of those who are already crowned with the glory of heaven.

We should appeal to her on this feast of Mary, Queen of All Saints. We should ask her to help us love her, to help us imitate her, to help us honor and appreciate her.

The people of the little town of Salency, France, yearly honor some young lady because of her virtue. So too every year on this feast the citizens of God's Church honor the one who stood above all men and all women in virtue and grace. Amen.

OUR LADY OF FAIR LOVE—May 31

"I am the mother of fair love, and of fear, and of knowledge, and of holy hope." Ecclesiasticus, 24:24.

Algiers is in North Africa. It is the location of a leper village. Some years ago an American tourist paid a visit to this colony out of curiosity. He noticed that a community of Catholic Sisters were caring for these outcasts. He was attracted particularly by one of these self-sacrificing women; her youth, her beauty, her evident refinement drew his attention. He discovered that she was an American girl. He sought an introduction and told her:

"Sister, I would not do this work for $10,000 a year."

"No," replied the Sister, "nor would I do it for $100,000, or even a million dollars a year."

"Really," said the stranger, "you surprise me. What then do you receive?"

"Nothing," answered the Sister, "absolutely nothing."

"Then, why do you do it?"

Sister lifted the crucifix hanging from her Rosary, kissed it sweetly, and explained:

"I do it for the love of Him, for Jesus who died for the love of men and for the love of me. In the loathsome ulcers of these lepers I see the wounds of my crowned and crucified Savior."

It is difficult to imagine a love greater than that of the sensitive woman who will leave home and comforts to bury herself in the service of people with running sores, depressed spirits, and a constant need of attention. The world admires such Christ-like service and love. Yet, there was another woman whose love for Christ was even greater than this. It was Mary, the Mother of Jesus. We call her Our Lady of Fair Love because of the unique and unexcelled love she had for God and man. On May 31 we celebrate the feast of that title, because Mary's love for her neighbor was heroic to a high degree. We also keep this feast in the hope that Mary's love of God and neighbor will serve as an incentive to us.

Love is a divine power which helps us to esteem God above all things for His own sake and our neighbors as ourselves for the love of God. Love is the fulfilling of the law. The command of charity is the first, the fundamental, the greatest command of Christ.

"Thou shalt love the Lord thy God with thy whole heart, and with thy whole soul, and with thy whole mind.... Thou shalt love thy neighbor as thyself." St. Matthew, 22:37-39.

Charity is a holy fire in the heart of man. Charity is the most necessary of the virtues. Without it nothing avails. With it everything becomes worthwhile in the eyes of God.

And Mary possessed this great virtue of charity in the highest, most eminent degree.

1. The love of Mary for God and neighbor was a matchless, a unique love:

   A. She kept her mind continually fixed on God. Other thoughts came to her, but always in the light of God's love.

   B. She directed all the desires of her heart, like darts, toward God. Human desires will come to human hearts; they must be directed, like Mary's, in the light of God's love.

   C. Mary directed all the sentiments of her soul toward God and neighbor. Our feelings and emotions are often wayward. If we direct them to God, we are fulfilling one phase of the love of God.

   D. Mary's life was not a string of interrupted acts of charity, such as we find in the lives of some saints, but her life was one continuous act of love. Our love is like a flower which we give piece-meal to Almighty God; Mary's love was like one complete flower, offered with one complete act of generosity.

2. Mary surpassed all others, not only in her love of God, but also in her love of neighbor. She had heard Jesus tell that the love of neighbor is the second wing of the love of God. St. John the Evangelist is the writer of love, which he learned not only from Jesus, but from long and tender association with the Mother of Fair Love. We see that love in Mary's conversation with the Archangel Gabriel; we see it when she learned that Elizabeth, her cousin, was expecting a child; and when she set out to visit this cousin and offer her services; we see Mary's thoughtful charity at the marriage feast of Cana; we see it in her anxious search for Jesus when He was lost in the temple; we see her love when she braved the boos and stares of the mob on the way of the cross; we see love in tears standing beneath the cross.

   That Mother love has continued through the centuries. It has been the inspiration of heroic deeds of charity in every age, in every land. Those women serving the lepers, not only in Algiers in North Africa, but throughout the world, and right here in our own United States, those women receive their inspiration from the example of Mary, the Mother of Fair Love.

3. Mary's love for her neighbor is a motive for our charity. It stimulates love. We see this constantly in the works of charity performed with the protection of our Blessed Lady. Hundreds of hospitals and asylums are run by the dynamo of Mary's love. Hundreds of thousands of consecrated women give their lives to serving the sick and the poor and the orphans and the aged, yes, and the leper. They give up everything; many give up even their own name, and take instead the name of some saint, prefixing it with the name of Mary, because she is the inspiration of the love they show towards Christ's needy ones.

   Mary is an inspiration to you and to me in daily life. When a thought, word or act of charity is in order, or is called for, think of our Blessed Mother, and charity will become second nature. Love and charity after the model of Mary is not laborious. It is fair and beautiful—here and hereafter, when the Mother of Fair Love will smile her approval. Amen.

MOST PURE HEART OF MARY
(Saturday after the Octave of Corpus Christi)

"Behold the handmaid of the Lord; be it done to me according to thy word." St. Luke, 1:38.

This story comes to us from Dublin, Ireland. Fritz Kreisler, the world famous violinist, had completed a concert one wintry evening in 1932. As he stepped into his car, he heard someone playing a fiddle in front of the theatre where he had just given his concert. It was an Irish girl named Lillian Mack. She was playing on the sidewalk for pennies.

For several minutes Kreisler listened intently. He then asked the girl to call at his hotel. There she played for him again, and he was so much taken with her ability and her sense of artistry, that he later asked her to sign a contract to give a concert at the Theatre Royal.

Here was an artist, a world famous musician, who recognized in a simple, humble little girl a kindred sense of beauty, an ability to play a sort of harmony that fitted in with his own, an ability which made it possible for her to leave the street and play upon the stage before admiring crowds.

In a similar way Almighty God, the Artist of the universe, picked out one whose heart was in tune with His own, a poor, humble maiden named Mary. He chose her from all the women of the world to be the Mother of His Son.

Next Saturday we celebrate the feast of the Most Pure Heart of Mary, a feast that is expressive of the holy harmony between the heart of Mary and the heart of God. To realize the beauty of Mary's heart, we want to consider that heart in itself; we want to consider how her heart was united with God; and we want to point out the love of Mary's heart for men.

1. In itself the heart of Mary was excellent. The heart is the center of the emotions; at least it registers our emotions. The heart is one of the most powerful organs of the human body. It is one of the greatest creations of God. It is a source of awe and admiration to those who understand its workings. Certainly God must have been pleased with the creation of the heart of man.

How much more must God have have been pleased with the heart of Mary that was so much in harmony with His own. Exery human heart has been stained with sin, but the heart of Mary was without any sinful stain. For that reason her Pure Heart was especially pleasing to the Almighty.

Some writers and theologians have explained that when we speak of the Most Pure Heart of Mary we do not mean pure virginity alone, because we have two other feasts to honor her purity—that of the Immaculate Heart of Mary on August 22, and of the Purity of the Blessed Virgin on October 16. Next Saturday's feast goes above and beyond purity and chastity to speak of Mary's universal goodness.

The Most Pure Heart of Mary was the nursery of all the virtues. We see there humility, detachment, lively faith, complete submission to the plans

40

of God. In that heart we see a burning charity, courage, constancy, and every other virtue in the highest degree.

2. The heart of Mary was in harmony and union with God:

   A. From all eternity God had chosen one who He knew would be in perfect harmony with His plan. As a little girl she went out from the affection and protection of her family to live and serve in the temple of the Lord, to give herself completely to Him.

   B. In God's good time she left the temple and in her tender teens is told that she is to be the Mother of God. In this she is united with the Third Person of the Trinity in particular, as St. Luke so beautifully describes it.

   C. And Mary was united with the Second Person of the Blessed Trinity, Jesus Christ. She had the privilege of giving Him His human nature, of being united with Him for several months in that closest human bond, that of mother and unborn child. In these ways the Heart of Mary was perfectly in harmony with God the Father, God the Son, and God the Holy Spirit. That is why we honor her Most Pure Heart.

3. We honor the Most Pure Heart of Mary because of its love for us. The highest expression of love is the gift of something you love to the one beloved.

The Holy Spirit emphasizes God's love for man by saying: "God so loved the world that He sent His only begotten son." God's best gift was Jesus. And Mary's best gift was Jesus. God's love echoed in the heart of Mary.

4. At the Annunciation Mary realized that her Son was to be the Redeemer. She realized that meant a sword of sorrow would pierce her heart. She realized all the difficulty, the calumnies, the outrages, the thorns, the nails, the cross. Her heart consented to it all, in harmony with God's plan.

5. Finally, beneath the cross Mary made her complete offering and sacrifice, in union with the desire of the heavenly Father.

Like a skilled violinist Mary played along in harmony with the Divine Artist. You have all heard of George Elliot, whose real name was Maria Evans. She was reared a Methodist, but died an atheist. This woman who hardly could be expected to do so, paid the following touching tribute to the Heart of Mary:

"Heart of Mary, bless the way,
"Keep us all by night and day.
"Heart of Mary, Mystic Rose,
"Send us all a sweet repose.
"Heart of Mary, Morning Star,
"Ward off danger, near and far.
"Heart of Mary, by thy sorrow,
"Keep us upright through the morrow.
"Heart of Mary, by thy grace,
"Give us with the saints a place." Amen.

"I will put enmities between thee and the woman, and thy seed and her seed: she shall crush thy head, and thou shalt lie in wait for her heel." **Genesis, 3:15.**

A great sinner one day came to St. Bernard, and with deep sorrow of heart confessed many serious sins. Then he exclaimed sadly and despairingly: "It is impossible for me to obtain forgiveness and find grace with God."

But the kindly St. Bernard told the man: "Not so, my son, you have no reason to despair: for, if you fear to find grace with God, hope still that you may find it with Mary. It is not in vain that she is called full of grace; the angel of the Lord has so designated her."

As he said these words the saint opened the Bible and looked for the passage in St. Luke where the angel addressed the Blessed Virgin in these words: "Do not be afraid, Mary, for thou has found grace with God." St. Luke, 1:30.

The saint went on to explain:

"Do you understand these words, my son? Mary has found grace. How so? Did she ever lose grace, to necessitate her finding it again? God forbid! But one can find what others have lost. Behold, it is you who have lost the grace of God by sin, and Mary has found it. Therefore, tarry not, despair not, arise, and go to the Mother of grace, prostrate yourself before her, and say to her:

" 'Mother of divine grace; ah, behold me, a wretched being. I have lost divine grace and thou hast found it. Mother, dear Mother, restore to me this lost treasure. Obtain for me the grace of reconciliation with thy divine Son and for the future be my protectress and support that I may not sin again and wantonly trifle with the gifts of my heavenly Father.' "

On June 9 we celebrate the feast of Mary, Mother of Divine Grace. Grace is one of the greatest and most important things in the life of a Christian. In fact, it is the life of a Christian. We call Mary the Mother of grace because God gave her the fullness of graces even before her birth, because she mothered Jesus Christ, in whom are all the treasures of wisdom and grace.

1. God gave Mary the fullness of graces before her birth. He had destined her to be the Mother of His Son, and therefore He adorned her with every possible privilege and beauty. Just as King Solomon, when he built the temple for the Lord at Jerusalem, used the most precious wood, and the most precious stones, just as he covered the inside with the best of gold even to the very nails, which were of solid gold, as we read in the Third Book of Kings, Chapter 6, so Almighy God, when He prepared a human dwelling for His Divine Son, spared no privilege, no grace, no beauty in adorning that dwelling. That is why the angel greeted Mary: "Hail, full of grace."

Furthermore, God would favor His Mother more than all others with regard to grace, because they are all still servants.

2. The Catholic Church greets Mary as the Mother of Divine Grace, because she continually increased in grace. Yes, she possessed the fullness of grace from the very first moment of her existence, but that life of God in her was capable of increase, and she did increase in God's grace. She was not defiled by original sin, and as a result Mary was not defiled by concupiscence. She had no obstacle to overcome in the way of sanctity. Some have said that in one day she made greater progress in holiness than the saints accomplished during the whole course of their lives. She cooperated with grace; she worked with grace; she lived in grace.

There was no self-love. There was no love of the world in Mary's love for God. Accordingly everything she did became a new source and cause of grace. Because of this most perfect love which Mary had for Almighty God, she referred everything to the heavenly Father, even the most insignificant action. As a result, every word, every step, every breath, every look, every gesture, every thought of our Blessed Mother was a new grace, in fact, an increase of grace.

For that reason spiritual writers call Mary a sea of graces. It is an apt figure, because, just as we cannot count the drops of water in the sea, so we cannot count the graces which Mary received and which she won for herself.

Here too Mary is your model—in seeking to increase within you sanctifying grace—the life of God in your soul. Every day opportunities are offered for us to grow in the love and in the life of God so that we might attain a higher degree of happiness in heaven. Every thought, word and action of every day is a means and a stepping stone to a spiritual life.

3. We call Mary the Mother of Divine Grace because she conceived and brought forth Jesus Christ, in whom are all the treasures of wisdom and grace, and in whom dwelleth all the fullness of the Godhead.

Every saint receives certain graces, graces to convert and to save souls, but Mary received the fullness, so that she might work for the salvation of all souls.

Because Mary is the means or channel of God's grace to us. St. Bernadin of Siena, the eloquent Franciscan preacher, used this striking figure:

"The Blessed Virgin is the neck of our Head through which all spiritual gifts are communicated to the mystical body of her Son."

We know that grace, the life of God in us, is absolutely necessary for salvation. We know that Mary is the Mother of that grace. To her we will go in prayer and devotion, begging for this life in abundance. Amen.

OUR LADY OF PERPETUAL HELP—June 27

"He who is mighty has done great things for me, and holy is his name."
St. Luke, 1:49.

Devotion to the Blessed Virgin as Our Lady of Perpetual Help took its origin in a picture by that name. Since June 27 is the feast of Our Lady of Perpetual Help, it will be interesting to recall the story of that famous picture. Some say it was painted by St. Luke, but it is now generally admitted that the picture was painted in the thirteenth century. It represents Mary and the Child Jesus with the Archangel Michael and the Archangel Gabriel offering the instruments of the passion. Here is the story.

At the end of the fifteenth century there lived in Crete a Christian business man. He was afraid of the Turks. He and some friends set sail for Rome, taking the painting with them. A terrible storm blew up, threatening to destroy their ship. But the crew and passengers prayed before the coveted canvas. They were saved. When this business man was near death in Rome, he willed the picture to one of the Roman churches, where it was exposed for veneration in 1499. For three hundred years the people honored the artist's conception of Mary as helper. Many favors and miracles were obtained.

Finally, in 1812, the French Army took possession of Rome. They also took possession of the picture. It disappeared when the church in which it was kept was destroyed. For forty or more years not a trace of it was found until one day it was discovered and given to the Redemptorists. On April 26, 1866, it was brought to the church of St. Alphonsus, where Pope Pius IX himself was one of the first to visit the new home of the famous image. He had it solemnly crowned June 23, 1867, and about ten years later granted a proper Mass and Office for the feast of Our Lady of Perpetual Help, as the picture was then and has ever since been called.

Take a close look at Our Lady of Perpetual Help. Notice her eyes— entreating, even begging us to come to her in all our miseries. Yes, those eyes are an answer to the prayer in which we ask Mary to turn her eyes of mercy toward us. The painter made her lips small to show that Mary spoke but little, yet when she did speak, she spoke wisely and kindly.

At the top of the painting, on either side, are four large Greek letters M P O U, which mean Mother of God. Over the Child there are four small letters I C X C, which mean Jesus Christ. The Greek letters over the angel, who holds a spear and a reed with a sponge on it, instruments of the passion, show that it is the Archangel Michael. The other blessed spirit with the cross and the nails is the Archangel Gabriel.

The Divine Child is represented as beholding a vision of His passion. In fact, He is so terrified at the sight of the cross that, in striking out his right foot, His sandle slips off. That is one of the odd parts of this picture. At the same time He clasps His Mother's hand, teaching us to go to her in every need. In this picture we see the story of Our Lady of Perpetual Help.

1. That business man and his companions who honored Our Lady of Perpetual Help obtained safety on a perilous journey. On our journey to

heaven we can obtain spiritual and material protection from Mary under this title.

2. Looking at this picture, we notice the right hand representing the power of our Blessed Mother. That hand is ever reaching out to her children. Whatever their need, Mary is there with her perpetually helping hand. With the grace and power God gives, it even works miracles.

3. In the eyes of Mary we see so much—her desire to help us, her desire that we come to her and ask her help. We see there her pity for our needs of body and soul. Those eyes draw us to her.

4. When we take note of Mary's lips, small, and expressive of the few words she spoke, we realize that most of her speech was directed to God, but that some of it was for our edification and instruction, like the text I have quoted:

"He who is mighty has done great things for me, and holy is his name." St. Luke, 1:49. Those words are from the Magnificat, the song Our Lady sang in glorifying the Lord who had done so much for her.

5. Take note of the four large Greek letters which mean Mother of God. Mary is the Mother of God, not in the sense that she herself is a goddess, but in the sense that she was the Mother of Jesus who was both God and Man.

6. We note also the words "Jesus Christ" over the Divine Infant, telling us that this Child, yes, this helpless Child, was really the Son of the great God, the Son who had come to save and redeem all men, who had come to this earth to set an example and to offer us the means of salvation.

7. The two angels remind us that the Infant Christ and His Blessed Mother foresaw the passion and death, the instruments that caused the terrible tortures of Christ's passion and crucifixion. Very cleverly the painter has represented this by showing the right foot of Jesus with the sandal slipped off and hanging by one of the straps, to show a child's human fear of torture and suffering.

8. Lastly, when we see Christ's hand in the hand of His Mother, we have the whole significance, the best lesson of this famous canvas. Jesus Himself is reaching for the hand of His Mother, as He no doubt often did as a Child and growing Boy, and later as a young man. Here Jesus sets us an eternal example, an every-day example—that we too should put our hand into the hand of Our Lady of Perpetual Help. Amen.

VISITATION—July 2

"Blessed art thou among women and blessed is the fruit of thy womb."
St. Luke, 1:42.

In her book, THE MAKERS OF FLORENCE, Mrs. Oliphant describes Albertinelli's picture of the "Visitation" in the Uffizi Gallery. Under an overhanging, vine-clad porch, with the blue heaven as a background, Elizabeth welcomes with a lovingly eager gesture the modest Mother of our Lord. The power of that picture to appeal to a lonely heart Mrs. Oliphant tells in these words: "I have heard of a woman, sadly lonely in a strange country, and little aware of the merits of the picture, poor soul! who would go and linger in the room 'for company,' wistfully wishing that the kind, penetrating, sympathetic tale of that old tender Elizabeth could fall on herself."

That lonely woman was none other than Mrs. Oliphant herself. How poignant the passage becomes when we know that. To her the picture, the remembrance of the visit of Mary to Elizabeth was a source of comfort, company, and cheer, yes, even of joy.

To us the memory of the Visitation will be the same. It was a happy visit, it was a joyful visit, it was a loving visit, a visit undertaken with love and friendship, a visit that brought many blessings to all concerned, a visit whose recollection will bring blessings to us.

We try to recall that joy when we pray the second decade of the Franciscan Crown: "The Immaculate Virgin Mary joyfully carried Jesus visiting Elizabeth."

After some time spent in serene and blissful thought of what had happened to her at the Annunciation, the Maid of Nazareth recalled what the angel had said about Elizabeth, her cousin. She decided to visit her. With a few friends Mary set out for the distant home of Zachary and Elizabeth, who were not only close kin, but also close friends.

The trip was long and tedious. Some say it took seven days. It was a dangerous journey, because of robbers and wild animals. But certain circumstances made it predominately a joyful journey. It was undertaken in springtime, when the Holy Land is gorgeously rich in nature's splendors. We can see the budding flowers raising their dainty, fragrant heads to greet her. We can catch the perfume of the blossoms as they cast their incense in her pathway. We can hear the birds caroling and heralding her passing, swooping back and forth and round about her, keeping her melodious company. We see the tall grass part as a curious rabbit peeks out to look. We spy a chipmunk scampering almost under her feet.

All nature is alert and eager to honor its Queen as she smilingly steps along the sylvan pathway, and over the wind-swept hills, joyfully carrying the glorious King of nature in her bosom. How happy she was, and how justly proud! How carefree and yet how contemplative! The fragrance, the melody, the color, the action, the aliveness all about her she realized were tributes to their God within her.

When she finally caught sight of the houses of Hebron, she stopped at a roadside spring to wash off the dust of the journey, to prepare to meet her cousin. We will let St. Luke report that meeting, Chapter 1, verses 39 to 49:

"Now in those days Mary arose and went with haste into the hill country, to a town of Juda. And she entered the house of Zachary and saluted Elizabeth. And it came to pass, when Elizabeth heard the greeting of Mary, that the babe in her womb leapt. And Elizabeth was filled with the Holy Spirit, and cried out with a loud voice, saying,

'Blessed art thou among women and blessed is the fruit of thy womb! And how have I deserved that the Mother of my Lord should come to me? For behold, the moment that the sound of thy greeting came to my ears, the babe in my womb leapt for joy. And blessed is she who has believed, because the things promised her by the Lord shall be accomplished.' "

It was then Mary broke forth into her jubilant song, THE MAGNIFICAT:

"My soul magnifies the Lord,
    and my spirit rejoices in God my Savior;
Because he has regarded the lowliness of his handmaid; for, behold, henceforth all generations shall call me blessed;
Because he who is mighty has done great things for me."

Mary's joy infected all who heard her. Mary's smile reflected in the faces of all who saw her. Mary's happiness leapt to the hearts of all who came near her. The Mother of God brought joy to all whom she had come to visit, joy to all who received her, just as she ever brings joy to all who welcome her, to all who honor her.

Often during that three-months' stay Elizabeth drew her sweet, young cousin Mary aside to talk, as women will, about Mary's husband, Joseph, about his attitude toward what had happened, to discuss relatives and friends and household affairs, and the thousand things expectant mothers make conversation about.

Sweetly and knowingly Mary made answer, expressing complete confidence in the man whom God had given her for a partner. She appeared not in the least disturbed or anxious about material considerations. Instead she turned the talk to eternal topics, to the praise of God's goodness, to thanking the Almighty for His kindness to her, to the future work of the wonderful Child she carried in her womb. Her soul soared above earthly concerns to a world of spiritual happiness.

That happiness she wants us to share. That happiness we do partially share as we slip through our fingers the beads of the second decade, as we slip through our hearts the roses of prayer which they represent. We begin to share her bliss when we think prayerfully of how happy she was.

How happy the maiden visitor in her absolute trust in God. How happy she was to hear Zachary, his speech restored, singing the praises of God. How happy she was to think of the child John, future herald of her own Divine Son. How happy she was to see the happiness of her aged cousin thus singularly blessed by the Almighty. How happy to dream of holding her own Child in her own arms. How happily the days slipped by until happily she returned to Nazareth, joyfully centering all her attention upon Jesus within. Amen.

OUR LADY OF MOUNT CARMEL—July 16

"I am the mother of holy hope." Ecclesiasticus, 24:24.

Some years ago that meaty magazine THE LIGUORIAN brought us this story. A large ship sailed from Marseilles, France, to a mission in Leberville. It carried many articles needed at the mission—books, linens, food, stationery, and gifts from friends. A canoe-load of native boys came out to meet the ship. Some of these were sons of savages and had just been newly baptized. One lad was just about to lift a large chest into the canoe, when one of the ship's officers demanded disdainfully:

"Tell me, Blackie, what is that little piece of cloth you are wearing around your neck."

"That, sir," came the respectful answer, "is a scapular."

"Scapular!" mocked the officer.

"And you, sir," asked the boy, "what is that braid on your sleeve?"

"That, stupid, is the mark of my naval rank."

"Good," said the boy. "Braid on your sleeve means that you are a commander; and the scapular on me means that I am a Christian, a Catholic and a soldier of Our Lady. I was confirmed last month."

The officer had nothing to say as the group around smiled and even laughed. But he was fair-minded. He gave the boy a coin and exclaimed:

"You are a clever youngster; after all, you are right."

The Feast of Our Lady of Mount Carmel, which we keep on July 16, takes its name from Mount Carmel in Palestine where some hermits centuries ago formed an order called Brothers of Mount Carmel or Carmelites. They were the first to celebrate this feast, which later spread throughout the Church.

Devotion to the scapular of Our Lady of Mount Carmel is intimately bound up with the feast of that name. The story of that scapular is interesting. Over seven hundred years ago St. Simon Stock, Carmelite General Superior, established the Confraternity of the Scapular in order to unite the devout clients of the Blessed Virgin in certain spiritual exercises.

Our Blessed Lady appeared to him on the night between the fifteenth and sixteenth of July in 1251. St. Simon reported the vision to his community at Cambridge, England, describing how our Blessed Lady herself gave him the scapular. Surrounded by a brilliant light, she offered the scapular to St. Simon, saying:

"Take, beloved son, this scapular of thy order as a badge of my confraternity and for thee and for all who wear it a special grace; whoever dies in this garment will not suffer everlasting fire. It is the sign of salvation, a safeguard in dangers, a pledge of peace and of covenant."

Imagine the joy and affection of St. Simon when he received this heavenly stamp of approval on his efforts. From that moment he strove with untiring zeal to announce the glories of Mary to the world, and to persuade all people to wear her scapular. Thousands eagerly embraced this uniform of Our Lady. Children, youth and parents, public officials, soldiers and sailors, hurried to enroll under Mary's protection. The Popes promoted the devotion. Pope Benedict XV declared:

"All should have a common language and a common armor: the language, the words of the Gospel; the common armor, the scapular of the Virgin of Carmel, which all ought to wear, and which enjoys the singular privilege of protection, even after death."

Put aside all superstition with regard to the scapular. It is wrong to believe that this piece of cloth, of itself, will protect you from spiritual and physical dangers. Every informed Catholic knows that it is up to God to allow the scapular to be an effectual means of avoiding evils and dangers. Furthermore, it would be wrong to expect that the scapular would prevent you from an unhappy death. It is a means to a pious, prayerful life, and that in turn is the means to a happy death. Nevertheless, it is certain that Catholics who wear the scapular with devotion and thought will be protected by the Blessed Virgin in a special way. Through her prayer they will receive many graces in life and at the moment of death.

People of the world are glad even to merely know, let alone to be friends of, those in position and power, whether in society or in the business and professional world. How honored are they who wear a garment given by the Queen of Heaven as a sign of salvation, a safeguard for body and soul, a pledge of peace with God and man.

2. The scapular is a means of obtaining God's graces and blessings. It is not the two little pieces of brown cloth sewn together that have any special value in themselves. They represent a holy habit. They represent Our Lady and dispose her to favors toward her devoted children. The scapular is a visible sign that the wearer honors Mary, the Mother of God. It is something that can be felt by the wearer and seen by the beholder. It is a continual, tangible reminder that Mary is our Mother.

3. Just as that little black boy in a far-off mission field realized that the marks on the sleeve of an officer, a naval officer, are the marks of his rank, so too, the Catholic realizes that the scapular is a mark, a visible sign that he is a member of the army, the family of our Blessed Mother, that he is a member of her own group, and that she in a special way is interested in those who wear her uniform, the badge and pledge that Our Lady of Mount Carmel will protect them. Amen.

HUMILITY OF OUR LADY—July 17

"He has regarded the lowliness of his handmaid." St. Luke, 1:48.

During a famine of the last century in lower Germany a rich man, who had a heart for the sufferings of the people, particularly for the hunger of the children, invited twenty of the poorest boys and girls of the village to come to his home. He told them:

"In this basket is a loaf of bread for each one of you; take it home and come every day at this same hour until the famine is over."

The children made a rush for the basket, doing quite a little pushing and quarreling. They rushed away without even thanking the donor. However, one little girl by the name of Frances stood aside until the very last, content with the smallest loaf. She kissed the hand of the man who gave the bread.

Next day the children acted in the same way, rushing to take the largest loaf and then rushing away. Again the smallest loaf was left to Frances. She brought it home to her sick mother who began to cut it. A number of coins fell to the floor. The frightened mother thought the money got into the bread by mistake. She told Frances to hurry back and give it to the good man. But the generous donor told the little girl:

"No, no, it is not a mistake. I put the silver in the smallest loaf to reward you. Continue to be unselfish, contented and grateful, and God will always bless and provide for you."

Just as the highest buildings have the deepest foundations, so the highest virtues must have as their foundation the deepest humility. Hence, we are not surprised that the towering virtues of the Blessed Virgin had for their foundation a deep and strong humility. Her humility inspires our admiration. It was a humility that God rewarded, somewhat as the generous donor of our story rewarded the humility of little Frances, who was content to take the last loaf. Because Mary put herself last, God chose her to be the first among all women, the one privileged to bear the Son of God. She was humble in every circumstance of life, but we would like to point out three phases of Mary's humility, as we approach the feast of the Humility of Mary, celebrated on July 17.

We see Mary's humility in the fact that she kept silent about the great mystery, the tremendous privilege which was given to her. We see Mary's humility in her reaction, in her words, at the time when the angel told her that she was to be the Mother of God. We see Mary's humility in the obscurity, the hiddenness of her life.

1. Mary was humble at the Incarnation. The angel told her that she was full of grace, that the Lord was with her, that she was blessed among women. Mary was troubled; she felt unworthy. She was not fearful at the sight of the angel, but at his message. How could she, a poor, humble, working girl, be the one chosen from all women for the highest honor of womanhood—to be the Mother of the Messias?

She even declared: "Behold the handmaid of the Lord." Yes, Mary was so humble that she would have been willing to work as a maid in the home of the Redeemer. As a reward for such profound humility she was chosen to be God's Mother.

2. Mary did not run from neighbor to neighbor telling of the wonderful privilege that was given to her. She kept it a secret. Yes, she had seen an angel. She had heard the angel tell her that she was blessed among all women. She had learned God's secret, God's plan. Mary kept all these wonders in her heart. She spoke no word, betrayed no emotion, revealed no secret; she remained humble, though chosen for the highest goal of womanhood.

Mary knew that the God hidden in her womb was the Creator of heaven and earth. She knew that His birth would be announced by stars and angels. She knew that the Wise Men would come to honor her Child. She knew that the world would fall to its knees to adore her Son, yet she kept it all a secret.

And that keeping of her secret became heroic when her spouse, St. Joseph, realized that she was with child. Yes, there was suspicion, suspicion of the darkest dye, but Mary spoke no word to clear herself or to explain. She left that to God.

Again we see her heroism in keeping it all quiet during her visit to Elizabeth. Mary knew her Son was far superior to the son of Elizabeth. Yet, the more privileged Mother honored the less privileged.

3. Her hidden life is another proof of Mary's humility. Almost entirely through the public life of Christ, as Christ was acclaimed and applauded, as He healed the sick, gave sight to the blind, hearing to the deaf and speech to the dumb, His Mother remained in the background. She was living a poor, yet happy hidden life. Yet, though she did not share in His glory and fame, she did share in His sufferings and death, she did follow Him on the way of the cross, she did stand beneath His cruciform deathbed.

True, Mary shared in the glory and joy of the resurrection and the coming of the Holy Spirit, yet even there she is mentioned last.

This humility of Mary is joined to a fullness of grace. We expect that she who was to have the highest role of womanhood, that of bearing and rearing the Son of God, would have every possible beauty and grace and virtue. Mary had grace in abundance. The only way we can express it is in the greeting of the angel: "Hail, full of grace."

Her merits were also of the highest degree. By her faithfulness with God's inspiration, she increased in grace. Still she was content to be a mere maid.

With all sincerity she could sing:

"He has regarded the lowliness of his handmaid."

On July 17 we will praise Mary's humility and beg her to help us be humble. Amen.

MOTHER OF MERCY (Saturday before the 4th Sunday of July)

"By me, his handmaid, he hath fulfilled his mercy which he promised to the house of Israel." Judges, 13:18.

For a whole year the town of Calais, France, was besieged by the English, who lost many troops. Starvation finally forced the French to give up. But the English king, Edward III, would not accept their surrender unless six citizens of Calais came before him bare-headed, bare-footed, dressed in rough shirts, and each with a halter about his neck. He demanded the keys of Calais, and that these men accept his pleasure, however severe, before the rest of the citizens would receive mercy.

Imagine the sorrow of the besieged city. No one wanted to give his life in such a way. At length a nobleman by the name of Eustace de Saint Pierre spoke to the assembly:

"I will be one to offer my head to the King of England as a ransom to save this fair town from sack and spoil."

At once five others volunteered. They put on the rough shirts and halters. Bare-footed and bare-headed, they went before the English king who angrily reminded them of the terrible losses he suffered through their stubbornness. At last he ordered the six citizens to be beheaded. The king's noblest and bravest warriors pleaded with him to spare. But in vain. Then Queen Philippa arose from her seat beside the king, knelt before him, and with tears streaming down her cheeks, she prayed:

"My lord and husband, I have crossed the sea through many dangers to be with you. Let me now pray you to take pity on these six prisoners."

After a few minutes of deep thought the king declared:

"Madam, I wish you had been elsewhere this day. I cannot deny the boon you ask of me. Take these men and dispose of them as you will."

The gracious queen gave the six hostages better clothing, presented each with a certain amount of money, and had them safely brought back through the lines and set at liberty to return home.

There is a picture of Mary, Mother of Mercy, whose feast we celebrate on the Saturday before the fourth Sunday of July. Mary is in every sense a Mother of Mercy because she is the Mother of Christ, who brought mercy to the world. Mary is the Mother of Mercy for three special reasons:

1. She defends the sinner; 2. She tries to convert the sinner; 3. She receives sinners with joy when they repent.

1. Mary shows her mercy toward sinners by shielding them against God's anger and punishment. We have many types of this in the Old Testament, particularly that of Nabal, who refused aid to King David and his people when they were in need. Abigail, the wife of Nabal, appealed to her husband and did secure the needed aid. We have many such figures in the Old Testament of a queen or wife appealing on behalf of those who needed mercy.

In the "Hail, Holy Queen" Mother Church has taught us to address Mary as Mother of Mercy. We say that prayer after every low Mass. "Hail, Holy Queen, Mother of Mercy, our life, our sweetness and our hope." Mary appealed for sinners during her life; she still does from heaven. Into her mouth can be put the words of Sacred Scripture:

"I desire not the death of the wicked but that the wicked turn from his way and live." Ezechiel, 33:11.

Defending sinners is Mary's occupation, as it is the task of every queen to defend those who need mercy. The king takes care of the justice, but the motherly heart of the queen goes out to those who need mercy. Every sinner needs mercy. We need it. Mary has defended us. Otherwise, how could a wicked world continue to exist, or how could sinners continue to live under the wrath of God? Mary shields us by praying to her Divine Son for us, by holding back His avenging hand, by persuading Him to show further patience and mercy. She pleads with Him for us. She even promises that we will repent, that we will amend our lives and make satisfaction for our sins.

Yes, we appreciate this motherly goodness and mercy, but we must not abuse it. Should we be at this moment the objects of God's wrath, then this is the time to go to the Mother of Mercy. She will shield us just as Queen Philippa defended the six condemned men of Calais.

2. We call Mary our Mother of Mercy because she tries to convert sinners by sending her servants, particularly her priests, to exhort and guide and direct souls, to bring them back to the sacraments of Mother Church. She converts sinners by placing in their path a good book, a Catholic paper, pamphlet or magazine. She directs the sinner's gaze to a crucifix or to a picture of herself. She even goes to the King Himself, and, like Queen Philippa, begs God for mercy.

We have all heard the story of St. Augustine, who was converted by the prayers and tears of his earthly mother, St. Monica. But St. Augustine himself declared that his conversion was due, not so much to the tears and prayers of his earthly mother, as to the tears and prayers of his heavenly mother, Mary.

We must not presume upon that mercy, but betake ourselves to her motherly heart and make this mercy of God a permanent fact in our lives.

3. Mary is the Mother of Mercy because the conversion of sinners brings her so much joy. We know that there is joy in heaven over one sinner that does penance. Certainly there is joy in the heart of the Queen of heaven when a sinner repents. The Blessed Virgin once told St. Bridget:

"However much a man sins, if he returns to me with a real purpose of amendment, I am instantly ready to welcome him; neither do I pay attention to the greatness of his sins, but to the intention alone with which he comes. I do not disdain to anoint and heal his wounds, for I am called, and truly am, the Mother of Mercy." Amen.

OUR LADY OF THE ANGELS—August 2

"There was with the angel a multitude of the heavenly army praising God."
St. Luke, 2:13.

One of the greatest masters of fiction was a writer by the name of Henry Sienkiewicz. He has written three books filled with stirring stories of the constant devotion of his Polish countrymen to Mary the Mother of God. In one of these books entitled "With Fire and Sword," he tells this incident:

The Polish knights and their helpers are closely besieged at Zbarig. Pan Longin, the hero, volunteers to bring news of their need to the king. It was their only hope. After Confession and Communion, the hero starts out in the night on his desperate journey, a journey he was never to finish. He was careful, he was courageous, but that did not save him. He was detected and surrounded. The Tartars and Cossacks, in spite of their numbers and their desire to do so, were unable to capture him alive. They slew him with bow and arrow. Let the author tell the story:

"At sight of the bows and arrows . . . Pan Longin saw death was at hand, and he began to pray the Litany of the most holy Lady. It became still. The crowds restrained their breath waiting for what would happen. The first arrow whistled as Pan Longin was saying, "Mother of the Redeemer" and it scratched his temple. Another arrow whistled as he was saying, "Glorious Lady," and it stuck in his shoulder. The words of the litany mingled with the whistling of the arrows, and when Pan Longin had said, "Morning Star," arrows were standing in his shoulders, in his side, in his legs. The blood from his temples was flowing into his eyes; he saw through a mist the field and the Tartars; he heard no longer the whistle of the arrows. He felt that he was weakening; that his legs were bending under him: his head dropped on his breast. At last he fell on his knees, then he said with a half groan, "Queen of the Angels." These were his last words on earth. The angels of heaven took his soul and placed it a clear pearl at the feet of the Queen of Angels."

On August 2 we honor Mary as Queen of the Angels. On the wings of thought fly into the heavenly home. There you will pass by all the nine choirs of angels up to the very throne of God, to behold the queen of all these heavenly spirits. We can call Mary Queen of the Angels because she was more favored by God than all the angels. There is still another reason for calling her Queen of the Angels: she can and really does do more for our souls than the heavenly spirits ever could do. These spirits are the servants of God; but Mary is the daughter of God the Father, Mother of God the Son, and spouse of God the Holy Spirit. All through her life we see the angels about our Blessed Mother:

1. We see the Archangel Gabriel announcing to the Blessed Virgin that she is to be the Mother of God. This archangel salutes her, greets her, honors her, because the archangel realized that Mary was his Queen.

2. At Bethlehem we hear the angels announce the birth of the Son of God in a stable. "Glory to God in the highest, and on earth peace to men of good

54

will." Yes, there was with the angel a multitude of the heavenly army praising God. These angels were honoring their Queen, even though she was a humble, simple Jewish Mother. These heavenly messengers came from the throne of God to tell the world that this Child was really the Son of God.

3. Again the angels enter Mary's life when they warned St. Joseph to take the Child and flee into Egypt. What is the power of the sword, when the angels of God spread their wings to protect the Infant Son of God? The angels must have hovered protectingly about Our Blessed Mother and the Holy Family as they made their perilous, tedious trip to a foreign land, and also during their sojourn there.

4. Again the angels appear when our Lord was tempted in the desert. After His long fast the heavenly messengers bring Him food and consolation. Here we see the angels performing one of their most important duties, namely, to supply the wants of our bodies and of our souls. Mother Church tells us that they are ever guarding and watching over us, helping Mary to protect us.

5. There was an angel in the Garden of Gethsemani when Jesus suffered His agony. We read, "an angel from heaven appeared to him, strengthening him." St. Luke, 12:43. In a similar way God's angel comes to us with consolation when we bear sufferings and trials in the spirit of Christ. These spiritual friends are at our side in times of trial and in times of triumph, along with their Queen.

6. The angels were at the tomb. One of them rolled away the stone and then announced:

"Fear not, you, for I know that you seek Jesus who was crucified. He is not here; for he is risen, as he said. Come and see the place where the Lord was laid." They helped the Mother to see her risen Son.

7. Finally, on Ascension day two angels addressed the disciples as they looked at the departing Master:

"Ye men of Galilee, why stand ye looking up to heaven? This Jesus who was taken up from you into heaven shall come as you have seen him going into heaven." Acts, 1.

8. According to an unquestionable tradition of Mother Church, Mary was taken into heaven by the hands of angels. Thus, all through her life messengers of the Almighty waited upon her, honored her, and brought her messages.

We should have more devotion to these blessed spirits and to their Queen. We should listen to their inspirations and spiritual suggestions. Like that Polish hero of our story, Pan Longin, we too must honor the holy angels and the lovely Lady at their head. If a prayer to them is on our lips through life and especially in death, we can hope that we too will be assisted into heaven by the hands of angels.

Many paintings picture Mary surrounded by angels. Let those spirits remind you constantly that she is the Queen of the Angels. Amen.

OUR LADY OF THE SNOWS—August 5

"Thou art all fair, O my Love, and there is no spot in thee." Canticles, 4:7.

It was a sweltering August afternoon in Kansas. No breeze, no rain, no prospect of relief. A four-year-old boy, resting from his perspiring play, looked up at the heavens and exclaimed:

"Mommy, this would be a good day for it to snow."

Improbable as it is for snow to fall during August in the Midwest, legend tells of a snowfall that seemed even more impossible. Sixteen centuries ago, on August 5, 352, snow fell during the night in the least likely of places, Rome, where it seldom snows, where entire winters pass without a single snowflake. Here is the story:

There lived in the Eternal City a nobleman named John and his childless wife. They were of high birth and breeding, blessed with much of this world's goods, but never blessed with a child. To whom could they leave their estate and heritage? They chose the Mother of God as their only heir. But the problem was how to bequeath her all their belongings.

They prayed the Blessed Mother to make known some method or means of doing this. They even asked for some sign that they might be certain. In answer the Virgin Mother, during the night of August 5, appeared to John and his wife and also to the Holy Father, Pope Liberius, directing them to build a church in her honor on the crown of the Esquiline Hill. The sign? Snow will cover the crest of the hill.

The flakes fell silently during the night, blanketing the peak of the historic hill. Snow in August and in Rome! Quickly the news spread and quickly crowds gathered to throng up the hillside and behold the white wonder. When it became known that the snow was a sign from our Blessed Mother, the people spontaneously added another to her long list of titles; they called her "Our Lady of the Snows."

Ever since, through the sixteen centuries since the building of the basilica on the spot, the faithful from the far corners of the Christian world have made their way to St. Mary Major. It is the mecca of Mary's millions of children. It is one of the most popular churches in the world. Invoked there under the title "Our Lady of the Snows," Mary has been pleased to secure many and various blessings, as numerous and varied as the flakes of snow which fell that August night.

The church built by John and his wife, and restored and enlarged at various times in later centuries, was known by different names, chiefly as the Basilica of Liberius, who was pope at the time, and as St. Mary of the Crib, because there are preserved relics of the crib of Christ. In order, however, to distinguish it from the many other churches in Rome dedicated to the Mother of God, they finally decided to call this St. Mary Major. "Major," as you know, means greater. This is the greater or the greatest of the temples of God under the patronage of Mary. It is one of the four basilicas in which Holy Year pilgrims to Rome had to pray in order to gain the indulgence of the Holy Year.

Most fittingly do we call Mary, Our Lady of the Snows. The white blanket of that ancient August was a certain sign of the wishes of our Blessed Lady. That snow was also rich in spiritual meaning. We speak of Mary as being pure as the driven snow. It is a symbol of her greatest glory, her purity. We can also speak of the blessings and favors and graces obtained through Mary as being varied and numerous as the falling snowflakes.

Science tells us that every snowflake is different in its form and make-up. The varieties of size, outline, structure and ornamentation are almost without limit. No written description, not even the hundreds of pictures we may study in articles and books on snow, can possibly portray the wondrous beauty, the startling complexity, and the perfect symmetry of these congealed particles of moisture floating and dancing down from the sky. Science has not yet discovered all the wonders of these white birds fluttering to the earth, nor the many benefits these feeble flakes bring to the soil.

What a beautiful figure of the blessings Mary obtains for us! To begin with, her blessings come down from heaven, like the snowflakes. Like the snowflakes, the graces she obtains for us are varied—some large, some small. Some are given just for a time; others are lasting. Like a snowflake, every grace is a miracle in itself, something which we cannot appreciate or describe in words.

Snow changes the face of the earth: it will paint over a field of mud with a coating of white. The grace of God, won through prayer to Mary, also changes the face of the earth. Snow serves many useful purposes: it preserves the heat of the earth; it protects vegetation from the severe cold of winter; it supplies moisture with slow effectiveness. Grace serves similar purposes: it preserves the warmth of God's love in our hearts; it protects the soul from the chill of temptation and sin; it nourishes the soul with renewed divine life.

We see a further symbolism. There are millions living in lands of ice and snow who have not come to the knowledge of Mary and her Divine Son. We might ask that with the actual snowflakes she shower down upon them the graces of the true faith.

In particular, may that land where snow falls long and heavily, Russia, come to share in a fall of graces, through prayer to her whom we honor on August 5 as "Our Lady of the Snows."

Make this a significant feast by begging Mary to bestow her blessings upon yourself and upon the world. With the little four-year-old we can say to her on that feast:

"Mother, this would be a good day for it to snow." Amen.

REFUGE OF SINNERS—August 13

"For she is the brightness of eternal light and the unspotted mirror of God's majesty, and the image of His goodness." Wisdom, 7:25.

St. John Church, Cincinnati, Ohio, is in charge of the Franciscan Fathers. Every year for two decades and a half the people of the parish have staged a beautiful Passion Play. One Lent a young mother took her seven-year-old daughter to this pageant. Before the performance the mother explained as well as she could the great meaning of the passion.

The play went on to that tense moment when Judas in his despair cries out:

"To whom shall I go? I am forsaken by everyone. Oh, to whom shall I go?"

The little girl was sitting on the edge of the seat, wrapped up in the performance, thinking that everything was real. With a woman's sympathy she felt sorry for Judas. She felt that there must be something he could do. So, turning to her mother at that tensely dramatic moment, the little girl exclaimed in a clear, silvery voice that could be heard throughout the hall:

"Mother, why doesn't he go to Mary? She will help him, I know."

What that little girl said about Judas, the traitor, the thankless, ungrateful traitor, we can say to every sinner: Why don't you go to Mary? She will help you, I know.

Mary is the Refuge of Sinners; she has been called that through the centuries; she has proven herself to be the refuge of those who have offended the Almighty.

That is why on August 13 we celebrate a special feast under the title, "Mary, Refuge of Sinners." When we hear that title our thoughts go way back into the Old Testament. There we read of so-called cities of refuge. The pitying spirit, which even the old Jewish law showed toward criminals, established certain cities where those who had run afoul of the law might hide from the arms of authority. There were no less than six Levitical Cities, three on either side of the Jordan, where men who had been guilty of involuntary murder might find protection until they were released from banishment by the death of the high priest. These cities had the obligation of receiving the culprit and lodging him without charge.

In addition there were at least 48 other cities which had this same privilege of asylum, as it was called. Even the Greeks and Romans had their cities of refuge. Christianity had them too.

We read that the Middle Ages had the beautiful custom of offering, "the right of sanctuary" to those who had broken the law. Men could find refuge in a church or sanctuary. This humane and Christian custom of showing mercy to those who needed it, was finally abolished by the Church, because it led to great abuses and flouting of the law.

This showing of mercy to criminals was not in itself a defiance of law and justice. It was simply offering sanctuary and protection to those who had offended the law, men who might be punished by private vengeance.

It prevented what we call lynch law, or taking the law into one's own hands.

Instead of a city, a town or a district, we have today as a place of refuge the heart of a Mother, the heart of our Blessed Mother. To her we fly in every need. To her we fly in every need of repentance and sorrow and contrition and forgiveness.

1. Since Mary is the Mother of the Redeemer, the one Savior of all sinners, we can expect her to be merciful to sinners. She shared with Christ in the salvation of the world. From the crib to the cross Mary took part in the redemption. She caught Christ's spirit of forgiveness and mercy, even to the worst offender. It is impossible that such a Mother should show no mercy towards the violators of God's law.

And now that she is in heaven, where her power is greater, where she is close to the throne of the Almighty, we can expect that she will continue to show this mercy to those who offend Almighty God. We quote St. Peter Damian:

"Mary is powerful in heaven and on earth, and even those who are on the verge of despair she inspires with hope."

2. Mary is not indifferent to sin. She hates it. But like her Divine Son she loves the sinner, she loves the souls for whom Christ suffered and died, she prays for them continually.

3. In the Old Testament we find many figures of Mary as the refuge of sinners, like Ruth who "gleaned the ears of corn after the reapers." Ruth, 2:3. St. Bonaventure draws this comparison:

"As Ruth found grace in the eyes of Booz, so Mary found Grace before God. . . . The reapers are the gleaners in the vineyard of the Lord, the missionaries, preachers and confessors who endeavor to gain souls to God. But there are obstinate and hardened souls who do not allow themselves to be gained; these can be saved only through the powerful intercession of Mary. There is no sinner so corrupt and sunk in vice that Mary will despise and reject him. If such a one seeks help with her, she will most certainly reconcile him with Jesus and obtain pardon for him."

4. We have abundant proof that Mary helps in all needs of body and soul. She is especially willing to help in matters of salvation, in matters of forgiveness. St. Bernardine of Siena tells us:

"As the devil goes about seeking whom he may devour, so Mary goes about seeking whom she may save."

5. There is another appeal in having a mother as a refuge. Sometimes out of fear children hesitate to go to their father. But every child runs to its mother. Those who have offended God will much more readily go to the Mother of God.

6. To every sinner we say what the little girl said about Judas in the Passion Play:

"Why doesn't he go to Mary? She will help him, I know." Amen.

ASSUMPTION—August 15

"The Queen stood on Thy right hand in gilded clothing, surrounded with variety." Psalm 44:11.

Some years ago the world was agog with the crowning of King George and Queen Elizabeth of England. All possible pomp and pageantry were called into play. Those were days of festivity and celebration. Music and color and song and parade honored the newly-crowned heads of the Empire. Around the world press and radio flashed details of the ceremonies. Britain had a king and queen.

But there was a reception and a crowning of a Queen some twenty centuries ago that far surpassed the most elaborate coronation ever held on earth. When the Immaculate Virgin Mary was joyfully received by Jesus into heaven and there crowned Queen of heaven and earth, as we recall in the seventh decade of the Franciscan Rosary, there was a celestial celebration that exceeded beyond compare any similar ceremony ever held in the courts of men.

"Open the portals! The Queen is approaching. Lift up, O eternal gates!"

The choirs of heaven caroled her coming: "The Queen is coming. Here she comes."

The endless parade of the blessed crowded about the wide-open gates of heaven. There was tense expentancy, such as one finds along a line of march as a parade approaches. A roadway of clouds billowed the pathway from an uncorrupted grave to an incorruptible throne.

At last, borne by angels, the lovely Lady arrives. It is the first Assumption Day. The heavenly throng gasps with admiration. The celestial singers burst into song. The angels hurry to and fro to catch a glimpse of her and to tell their companions of her beauty.

Jesus waits at the open entrance, throws His arms about His Mother, leads her triumphantly and happily to the very throne of the heavenly Father, who leans forward and places solemnly and smilingly upon her beauteous head—the crown, as the Holy Spirit, heavenly Spouse of the Virgin Mother casts warmth and light upon the welcome newcomer.

Sweet scene of Mary's bliss! Who can measure her happiness? Who can count the throbs of joy in her heart: joy that now her lonesome life on earth without Jesus is over; joy that now she has Him, never again to lose Him; joy that now she can enjoy His company without the interruptions of earth or sense; joy that now she can help everyone on earth who is devoted to her Son; joy that she can now know the why and wherefore of many things that had happened to her here below; joy that she was forever to associate only with the good and pure and virtuous and kind; joy that now it is her turn, and it is in her power to show special kindness to all who had been kind to her while she walked this earth; joy that all the honor and all the praise and all the glory is given to her because of her Son; joy that the very crown she is wearing as the Queen of heaven and earth, is given to her because she is the Mother of Jesus, the Son of God; joy that an eternity is just beginning during which she can wrap herself in her Child and her Redeemer, even more closely than their lives had been entwined upon earth.

Happy hour and happy homecoming! Mary, we rejoice with you. We who still wander in this world, we who are weak and weary and all too worldly, we, however, who love to call you our Queen, who count upon your queenly protection, we, your children still upon this place of trial, we rejoice with you and with the angels and blessed and with the Holy Trinity. O newly-crowned Queen, now we have a Mother and Queen to look after us, a Mother most loving and a Queen most powerful. As with all your other joys, small as well as great, your going home, your being crowned, your being enthroned makes us happy. It makes those in heaven happy; it makes the heaven-hungry happy too.

Though bodily Mary was taken away from her children on earth, though bodily she seems far away, yet her leaving our planet must not make us lonesome. Rather, her Assumption and her Crowning should be to us a promise and an earnest of our own final glory with her. Her victory will be our victory. Until that day of triumph we will struggle on, knowing that always a Queen Mother is waiting and watching.

Who minds the discomforts and weariness of travel when he is going home to his mother? Who minds labor, who minds burdens, who minds delays, who minds sacrifices, when he is making his way to the place where mother lives?

Boys coming home from years of service abroad, youths riding buses and trains from college or work in a distant city, children coming home from vacation, will put up with every kind of convenience in the assurance that sooner or later they will be there—with mother.

That is how we feel about traveling on the roads of time, looking forward to meeting our heavenly Mother. Jesus and Mary are waiting to welcome us, waiting to receive us among the happy inhabitants of that heavenly home, waiting to reward us for the smallest service.

What joy that stirs up in our hearts! Look down, O Mother Mary, look down, O heavenly Queen, look down from the heights of thy glory, look down and be to us—and be to all—a loving Mother and a powerful Queen. Thank God for the joy that is yours today. Thank God for the happiness and hope it gives us to pray the prayer Christ Himself taught us, and then to salute thee ten times with your favorite greeting, the Hail Mary, as we think of your being received into heaven and crowned our Queen. Thank God everyone for this joyful Mother. Amen.

IMMACULATE HEART OF MARY—August 22

"Who is she that cometh forth as a morning rising, fair as the moon, bright as the sun, terrible as an army set in array?" Canticle of Canticles, 6:9.

Two widely separated incidents of recent years have a common significance. Separated by an ocean, these two happenings have a common meaning. The first: Los Alamos is a little town about 45 miles from Santa Fe, New Mexico. Of its 6,000 citizens, 3,000 are Catholic.

Los Alamos, you will remember, is the scene of the development of the atom. It is the atom bomb center of the world. Recently a new parish has been set up in this town, dedicated to the Immaculate Heart of Mary.

About the same time word came from Hiroshima, across the Pacific, the scene of the first atomic attack, that a new church was being built and would likewise be dedicated to the Immaculate Heart of Mary in memory of the many thousands who perished in that inhuman slaughter of innocents.

Yes, an ocean separates these two churches. Still, their dedication to the Immaculate Heart of Mary is prophetic. The atom is about the last word in the development of material and physical power. It can be a means of progress or a means of destruction. Hence it is appropriate that, in the place where the atom bomb was developed, and in the place where the first atom bomb was dropped, there be churches in honor of the Mary's Immaculate Heart.

Did she not, at Fatima in 1917, promise peace to the world through devotion to her Immaculate Heart? Yes, she asked for penance and prayer, but she also emphasized a third means for the saving of the world, namely, devotion and dedication to her Immaculate Heart. May we quote Mary's words to the children at Fatima, words also addressed to us:

"Our Lord wishes that devotion to my Immaculate Heart be established in the world.

"I want to ask for the consecration of the world to my Immaculate Heart and for the promotion of the practice of offering a Holy Communion of reparation to my heart on the first Saturday of the month.

"Repeat often, especially when offering an act of self-denial, 'O Jesus, I do this out of love for Thee, for the conversion of sinners and in reparation for the offenses committed against the Immaculate Heart of Mary.'"

What do we mean by devotion to the Immaculate Heart of Mary?

1. First, we mean devotion to her physical heart. Just as devotion to the Sacred Heart of Jesus is a special form of devotion to the Person of Christ, so devotion to the Immaculate Heart of Mary is a special form of devotion to Our Lady. In other words, we want to honor the entire person of Mary, not merely her heart. By devotion to that heart we promote love and esteem toward Mary. When we think of her physical heart, the heart of flesh, living and loving, a true Mother's heart, we are inspired to honor the entire Mary. We must never forget the heart that loved us so deeply during the years of her life on earth, the heart that beat in her holy breast at the greet-

ing of the angel, the heart that throbbed with joy at Bethlehem, the heart that supplied the Precious Blood of our Redeemer, the heart that was pierced with seven cruel swords, the heart that was broken beneath the cross, the heart now gloriously honored in heaven, the heart that always watches lovingly over all her children.

2. The second object of devotion to the Immaculate Heart of Mary is spiritual—it is devotion to the love of the Mother of God, a love which is symbolized by her heart. Right here we see the special reason for this devotion. Mary's heart is a symbol of love. It represents, it shows us, it reminds us of, the immense love of Mary for men.

3. A third and most important point is that this devotion is not an end in itself. Devotion to the Immaculate Heart of Mary is a means to an end, a means to grow in love and devotion to the Heart of Christ. That thought is expressed in the motto: "To the Sacred Heart of Jesus through the Immaculate Heart of Mary."

We can see three excellent reasons for promoting love for Mary's heart:

A. Man was not made to hate his fellow man, but to love him. The cure for the hate in men's hearts is found in the heart of the Mother of all men.

B. The world was not made to be destroyed in periodic baths of blood. The world was made to help man lead a fuller, richer life in union with God. There is a cure for war—the love in a Mother's heart.

C. Man was made to honor the name of God, not to dishonor it. Yet, today, disrespect toward the Almighty is world-wide. The very denial of the Divinity is the basis of the greatest threat to world peace today—Atheistic Communism. We will honor God when we learn to honor the heart of His Mother.

D. The Immaculate Heart of Mary is important because man is a creature having free will. He can choose between good and evil; he can direct his own actions. Mary will teach us how to make the proper choice.

E. How can we honor the Immaculate Heart of Mary?

1. By imitating the virtues that were centered there.

2. By reading and meditating about Mary, and praying to her.

3. By keeping the five first Saturdays.

4. By observing her feasts, especially the feast of the Immaculate Heart, August 22.

5. By placing her picture or statue in homes, workshops, and schools.

6. By joining groups that honor her.

7. By consecrating ourselves, our families, our organizations to her heart.

Then the atom bomb will not destroy the world. Rather, it will be guided by the love of Jesus and Mary for the benefit and blessing of mankind. Amen.

SEVEN JOYS—August 27

"My spirit rejoices in God my Savior." St. Luke, 1:47.

Robert Browning has given us an inspirational story in his poem "Pippa Passes." Pippa is an obscure but cheerful little Italian peasant girl. Almost every day of the year she goes to work in a noisy, stifling silk factory in a small Italian town perched among the purple Apennines. The poem describes her on New Year's day.

The whole day lies before her. With a merry, happy, innocent heart Pippa skips down the hillside and into the valley, singing as she goes. She seems to have the secret of perpetual cheerfulness, and all the green valleys in their green depths and the hillsides in their sunny heights are musical with her songs.

And all unconsciously, by the simple power of her cheerfulness Pippa keeps one man from committing murder and another from seducing an innocent maiden. One who is about to run away from his duty and his destiny, hearing her merry song of hope and trust in God and goodness, resumes his proper mission in the world. This cheerful, happy, joyful girl influences everyone she meets.

The gaiety of the innocent, the joy of Pippa is one of the great forces in the world which make for goodness. Cheerfulness is a religious duty.

On August 27 we celebrate the feast of the seven principal joys of our Blessed Mother. Mary had many joys, many moments of happiness and bliss. Her supreme joys were seven. The followers of St. Francis of Assisi honor those joys in the Seraphic Crown or Franciscan Rosary which has seven decades, each one of which is devoted to one of the seven great joys of Mary. On August 27 we remember those Seven Joys. This is how we Franciscans express them:

1. The first great joy of Mary was the Annunciation, which we Franciscans express in these words: "The Immaculate Virgin Mary joyfully conceived Jesus by the Holy Ghost." Read the account, clear, brief, and uplifting, in the first chapter of St. Luke, how the Angel Gabriel came from God and told the Virgin Mary that she was to be the Mother of God. Imagine the joy in the heart of Mary to learn from the messenger of the Almighty that she, who was willing to be but a handmaid or servant in the household of the Lord, that she was to be really the Mother of God. What joy and happiness at the greeting of the angel. What joy to know that now within her womb she carried the Son of God.

2. The second great joy of Mary was the Visitation. "The Immaculate Virgin Mary joyfully carried Jesus visiting Elizabeth." Charity and love inspired this visit. How happily our Blessed Mother must have made her way over the hills to the distant home of her cousin Elizabeth, who also was with child, the future John the Baptist. Womanlike, Mary wanted to tell her cousin and share in the joys of an expectant mother. What an inspiration and joyful example to all the mothers in the world.

3. The third great moment of joy in Mary's life was the Nativity. "The

64

Immaculate Virgin Mary joyfully brought Jesus into the world." Everyone who has ever experienced the bliss of Christmas has had just a faint echo of Mary's joy when she gave birth to Christ. Every mother shares that joy. Mary experienced it in all her innocence and sweetness. She experienced the holy happiness of bringing into the world the Son of God, who was to be the Redeemer and Savior of all men.

4. The fourth joy of Mary was that of the Epiphany, which we might express in these words: "The Immaculate Virgin Mary joyfully exhibited Jesus to the adoration of the Magi." Every mother is happy when she can show her child to others. Every mother is joyful when friends or acquaintances or even chance visitors comment about her child, praise it, and even bring it gifts. That was the happy experience of Mary when the three Wise Men came thousands of miles to adore and honor her Child, to bring gifts to her Boy.

5. The fifth great joy of our Blessed Mother she experienced when she finally found Jesus after His three-day loss in the temple. "The Immaculate Virgin Mary joyfully found Jesus in the temple." To have her child with her is a mother's joy. But to find a child that is lost is a greater joy because of the contrast to the sorrow of separation. Mary experienced such a bliss when she found Christ in the temple teaching and listening to the doctors, the learned professors of the law.

6. The sixth principal joy of the Blessed Mother was the one she experienced upon seeing Jesus after His resurrection. "The Immaculate Virgin Mary joyfully beheld Jesus after His resurrection." Words fail in expressing the happiness of the Mother of God when she saw her Son risen from the grave, saw Him in the full beauty of manhood, saw the Boy whom she had brought into the world, had reared and trained and taken care of for so many years. Her joy, by way of contrast with the grief of the first Good Friday, was supreme.

7. The seventh and crowning joy was that Mary had when she was taken up into heaven and crowned Queen of heaven and earth. "The Immaculate Virgin Mary was joyfully received by Jesus into heaven and there crowned Queen of heaven and earth." No human pen, no human brush can picture or express the joy in Mary's heart when she was finally reunited with her Son in the bliss of the beatific vision. Neither can we express in words the happiness in her heart when she was crowned, rewarded by her Divine Son who made her the Queen of this world and of the heavenly court.

These Seven Joys we honor on August 27. They are a source of joy to us. They remind us that joy is a note of Christ's Church. Joy is also a note and a fruit of our devotion to the Blessed Virgin. Amen.

HEALTH OF THE SICK (Saturday before last Sunday of August)

"He that shall find me shall find life, and shall have salvation from the Lord." Proverbs, 8:3.

Newton D. Baker was Secretary of War under President Wilson. He delighted in telling the following story:

During World War One he visited a certain hospital and found there a desperate and pitiable case. A young soldier had both legs shot away. One arm was gone. Both eyes were blind and his face was terribly battered and disfigured. No one expected him to survive.

Sometime later Mr. Baker met a friend who worked at the hospital.

"Did that young man live?" asked Baker.

"Did he live?" said the friend, "why, he married his nurse."

Baker admired this woman's heroism in loving someone in such a desperate situation. That nurse had nothing to gain from marrying that human wreck. After several years Baker had almost forgotten the incident.

One day, however, as trustee of Johns Hopkins University, he received a notice that the university, contrary to its usual custom, was conferring the degree of doctor of philosophy on a man named William Harrison Craig. The cabinet member discovered that this young man, despite almost insurmountable handicaps, had performed one of the most brilliant pieces of research work ever done at the institution. Imagine Secretary Baker's surprise when he found out that Craig, the man who was to receive this honor, was none other than the mutilated soldier he had seen some years before. When the legless and one-armed veteran was wheeled across the stage to receive the degree, the students and faculty arose to acclaim him. They cheered as they had never cheered before.

Back in Baker's mind was the thought of the nurse and the generous love that had helped this human being to live. He could not help thinking of the love that had given new hope to his sightless eyes, new strength to a mangled, crippled body.

In this generous-hearted nurse we see a figure of our Blessed Mother whom we honor under the title of Health of the Sick, on the Saturday before the last Sunday of August. Mary deserves that title for every reason. She was acquainted and familiar with the sick bed and the death bed.

1. The parents of Mary, St. Joachim and St. Ann, were on in years when their child was born. Dutiful daughter that she was, Mary, we may presume, took care of them in their feeble, old age.

2. The situation was similar with St. Joseph. In his own declining years Mary took care of him, especially as his last hour approached. Mary moistened his drying lips. She smoothed and fluffed his dying pillow. She kept watch through the night and day, folded his hands and closed his eyes in death.

3. But more significant still, Mary was the Mother of Jesus, the Divine

Physician. She saw Him healing the sick. She saw Him giving sight to the blind, hearing to the deaf, and speech to the dumb. She saw her Son restore the use of their limbs to those who were crippled. Mary saw Jesus healing the leper, and even raising the dead to life. She was the constant companion of Christ as He went about doing good. She saw Him not only healing souls, but also healing bodies, to prove that He was the Lord of life and death. She accompanied the Divine Physician constantly in His work of mercy.

4. On another score the title, Health of the Sick, is due to Mary. Throughout the world there are countless shrines dedicated to her, where the sick of every type find solace and often health. Outstanding among these is Lourdes in Southern France, a place where for a century millions have fled to find not only health of body but above all health of soul. And Lourdes is just one of an uncounted number of places where Mary has secured healing for the sick. In truth we can say that Mary builds her shrine beside every sick bed. She builds her shrine in every hospital and institution of mercy.

5. Mary deserves the title, Health of the Sick, because numerous organizations, societies and religious groups who serve the sick and the poor and the orphan and the leper, are dedicated to her. In the United States alone we have over 800 Catholic hospitals. The nuns who serve there take Mary as their nursing model. The women who have served in the wars of the world, those we call the angels of the battlefield, are dedicated to the service of the sick and wounded through the imitation of Mary.

6. Deeply as Mary is interested in the health of our bodies, just as her own Son was interested in freeing men from disease and sickness, our Blessed Lady is much more interested in the health of our souls. That is why we call her as St. Simon Stock did, "medicine of sinners." St. Ephrem called her, "Robust health for those who have recourse to her." Just as Jesus was concerned for the souls of men, so His Blessed Mother in her lifetime and ever since from heaven is interested in the health of human souls.

7. In another sense Mary is the health of those who are sick of soul. By her example, her virtues, her holy life she has led many out of the sickness of sin into the health of God's grace. By that same example she has saved many from ever getting sick with sin. A doctor or nurse who keeps someone from getting sick, does more than one who cures. Mary does both for sick souls.

8. In still another way Mary is the Health of the Sick. She witnessed suffering at its worst in the passion and death of her own Son. In her heart she felt the pangs and tortures and agony of His crucifixion. For this reason she is compassionate, understanding and sympathetic toward all who suffer. She suffered. Hence she understands suffering.

The nurse who took care of the crippled soldier in our story did something truly heroic. Mary does even more for the bodies and souls of her children. Amen.

MOTHER OF THE DIVINE SHEPHERD—September 3

"There shall be one fold and one shepherd." St. John, 10:16.

In Toledo, Spain, there lived years ago a nobleman by the name of Don Ranurez and his beloved wife, Donna Mercedes. After many childless years they were blessed with a Son who received at Baptism the name of Manuel. The pious mother at once took the child to the Chapel of Our Lady and dedicated him to our Blessed Mother with these words:

"O dear Lady of Grace, to thee I dedicate my child. Forsake him not, but preserve his soul from everlasting perdition."

Manuel grew up to be a strong boy. He was strong not only in body but also in mind. But as he grew through the teens he gradually lost his respect for religion until finally he believed neither in God nor in another life. The grief-stricken mother again went to our Blessed Lady, with this prayer:

"O dear Lady of Mercy, remember how I dedicated my unhappy boy to thee—remember he is therefore thine own child."

In her own way Mary heard the prayer of this pious mother. Manuel was taken dangerously sick, even to the point of death. He realized then that there was something beyond this life. He was sorry for his past, but when his health was restored he forgot about the things of eternity and went back to his sinful ways.

Not long after this both of his parents died, and Manuel lost all his money. He spent his time and funds in gambling and even used sharp, dishonest tricks that marked him as a cheat. He was compelled to leave the country to seek his fortune across the sea. Out on the ocean the ship took fire. The entire crew perished. The only one saved was Manuel who was lucky enough to find a plank and to float on it for a whole day and night. A vessel picked him up.

But the joy of being saved was drowned by the realization that his rescuers were pirates, and that he would be a slave the rest of his life. When the meaning and misery of this came fully to Manuel's mind, he put his face in his hands and groaned aloud. Just then a hand touched him on the shoulder and a gentle voice spoke to him in the language of his native land. He looked up to see a thin, worn old man in the brown habit of a follower of St. Francis of Assisi. This Franciscan priest, on his way to a foreign mission, had been taken into captivity. For a long time he had been a servant of the pirates. The troubled state of Manuel's heart was made known to the padre, who nevertheless contented himself with helping the body of Manuel. After a year of hard work, of suffering and danger, Manuel's respect for Father Fidelis became greater and greater. Gradually the teachings of his mother came back to him; the young man was sincerely sorry. One day he told the priest the whole story of his life. When he finished, the good padre exclaimed: "Truly, my son, your adventures are a fresh proof of the wonderful power of the Blessed Lady of Mercy. It is evident that the misfortunes which have come to you were but the means through which God wishes to draw you to Him even against your will."

In tears Manuel made his peace with God and bore his slavery with heroic patience. It wasn't long after this that Father Fidelis died. For three more years Manuel was held captive. At last he was given his freedom. He returned to Europe and entered a Franciscan monastery as a lay brother. There he led a holy life, spending as much time as possible singing hymns in praise of the Queen of Heaven.

1. This is just one of countless instances in history of the Blessed Mother being a good shepherdess herself, seeking after the lost sheep, using every means material and spiritual to bring a soul back to her Shepherd Son.

2. A shepherd, we know, is a man or woman employed in tending, feeding, and guarding sheep, especially a flock of sheep grazing at large. Figuratively, a shepherd is one who is charged with the religious guidance and care of others like a priest or pastor.

3. In many ways Mary is a shepherd herself, or a shepherdess. She was the Mother of Jesus who called Himself the Good Shepherd:

"I am the Good Shepherd." St. John, 10:11.

4. Mary is so interested and so influential in bringing and keeping souls in the flock that Mother Church celebrates the feast of Mother of the Divine Shepherd on September 3.

5. By her prayers and intercession Mary helps to bring in those who have strayed from the flock of Christ. Mary can say to thousands what St. Peter wrote: "For you were as sheep going astray, but now you have returned to the shepherd and guardian of your souls." I St. Peter, 2:25.

6. Mary helps bring in those who never were members of Christ's flock. True, many outside the Catholic Church criticize and complain that we pay too much attention to Mary, that we even adore her. At the same time Mary has drawn many into the Church. It is natural for all of us to honor our mothers. That is why many outside the fold are drawn to the true flock, to that flock where the Good Shepherd's Mother is honored and venerated.

7. There is a group of nuns, The Sisters of Our Lady of Charity of the Good Shepherd, who highlight this phase of Mary's interest. Their aim and purpose is to provide shelter for girls and women of sinful habits who wish to lead a truly Christian life. It is an inspiring sight to visit a Good Shepherd convent and see these nuns, encouraged by the Blessed Virgin, taking care of unfortunate girls, lost sheep who want to find the Good Shepherd. The inspiration of this heroic work is our Blessed Mother.

Should you ever stray, or should you know someone who has strayed, or someone who would like to belong to the true flock, appeal to the Mother of the Divine Shepherd, especially on September 3. Amen.

NATIVITY OF OUR LADY—September 8

"For she is more beautiful than the sun, and above all the order of the stars: being compared with the light, she is found before it." Wisdom 7:29.

Tom was ten, and Jane was eight, the eldest children of a fine Catholic family. Not much money in that family, but lots of love, the kind of love that makes children want to help their parents, the kind of love that prompts boys and girls to make little efforts to please their parents, the kind of love that moved Tom and Jane to think about giving their mother some gift on her birthday. But what should they give her? What could they give her? They had no money or means.

Talking and thinking it over, as such little men and little women will do, they decided to resort to what we might call a "racket," a scheme worked by many another child. To mother they went about a week before her birthday, and begged, yes, they begged from her a quarter. As if she did not know, mother asked what it was for, but the only answer she received was this:

"It's for something very, very special—special."

The birthday came. Imagine mother's "surprise" when there was thrust into her hands a neatly wrapped handkerchief with a big blue "M" embroidered on it. A little chorus sang soulfully, if not skillfully:

Happy birthday to you,
Happy birthday to you,
Happy birthday, dear mother,
Happy birthday to you.

Are you remembering that your Mother's birthday comes in September? Are you keeping in mind that September 8 is the birthday of the Mother of our Lord, the birthday of Mary, the mother of us all? Are you planning to give her a present? Have you thought of something to give her? Have you already picked a present that will please her? Have you some way to get it for her? Or, are you like myself and the rest of her children—wondering what to give, wishing you knew what she wanted, wishing you had some way to secure a really worth-while present for our Blessed Mother?

Let's try the old "racket," the plan that worked for Tom and Jane, the "racket" that you yourself may have used years ago on your earthly mother. Let us beg Mary, during these days before her birthday, to give us the things we know she will like to have us present to her on her birthday.

All mothers are alike. Like the mother of Tom and Jane, the Mother of us all will be glad to give us, will be glad to pay for the present we wish to give her. Mary will realize, as all mothers do, she will be paying for her own present, helping us to obtain a gift for her. She will enjoy the game.

Why not give her some gems and jewels? We can't afford such a gift, you will say. We can. We can give her the most precious jewel of them all—modesty. Purity of thought and word and action is the most precious

70

gem one could ever possess, yet it is a gift we can obtain only by begging it from our Blessed Mother. Ask her to give it to you, that you, in turn, might give it to her as a gift on her birthday.

We might ask her to give us the handkerchief of her tears, with a big, blue "M" upon it, signifying Mary; the tears of our sorrows and disappointments, our pains and misunderstandings, tears shed in her spirit of resignation, and into her very own handkerchief, which she will lend to us, that we might give it to her on September 8.

You mothers with babies, you have a particularly precious gift for Mary on her birthday. Why not offer your little one—and your big boys and girls too— to her on the eighth day of September?

Give them into her keeping. Wrap up their innocence in the arms of your motherly care, tie it neatly with the ribbon of prayer, and ask her to accept it. You might even make a little journey to church on Mary's birthday, and with your present in your arms, or kneeling at your side, dedicate and consecrate that bundle of goodness to God's Mother.

There is a very charming dress that Mary will like. It is delightfully plain and simple, wears well, is always becoming and is made of some very durable stuff called humility. Beg the materials of her, and with your own hand and heart, guided of course by Mary's skill, and modelled after her own deep humility, design for yourself and offer to her a deep desire to be accounted what you really are. How she will love it!

Women also love gloves. Mary would love a pair, if they are the gloves of charity, gloves for hands that are turning daily to some task of kindness, some deed of devotion, some act of love. If you ask her, Mary will help you find a pair that suits yourself. Then you can bestow them upon her as a gift.

Most mothers love flowers. Mary loves them. But how can we get flowers for her? God knew that His Mother would love to have flowers, even out of season, when He saw to it that the Rosary was established as a form of devotion to her. Need I remind you that saying the beads is weaving a garland, a circlet of roses for Mary? Present some of these imperishable blossoms to her on the anniversary of her birth.

Best gift of all will be Holy Mass and Holy Communion. In your heart on September 8 be like Tom and Jane. Beg these gifts of soul from Mary and then present them to her as gifts. Amen.

HOLY NAME OF MARY—September 12

"Thy name and thy remembrance are the desire of my soul: my soul hath desired thee in the night." Isaias, 26:8.

Some years ago a young lady called at the rectory after a mission sermon on the Blessed Virgin, in which I had urged my hearers to call upon the name of Mary in every trial, in every temptation and difficulty. Here is her story:

"This may sound like boasting, Father, but I'd like to tell you how the name of Mary helped me. My mother died about seven years ago. In her last days she told me many things, but one remark I'll never forget:

'Mary, remember you have the name of the Mother of God. Be true to that name.'

"She clutched my wrist as she said that, Father. I'm glad she did. It helped me to remember. Mary has really helped me. My older brothers and sisters married, leaving my younger brother and myself at home with dad. There was no one to watch me and warn me, but I've come through a lot of narrow escapes, thanks to God and His Mother Mary. Whenever I was in difficulties or doubt, I would think of the name of Mary—her name and my name. It always helped."

No doubt many another Mary could tell a similar story. Many another devoted to the name of the Mother of God can tell of strength and consolation and help obtained through honoring her holy title. When we honor the Holy Name of Mary on September 12 we are simply following the unwavering devotion of the Church from the dawn of Christianity.

This devotion is appealing and powerful. Who is this Mary and what does her name mean? There are about seventy different meanings for her name. The most appealing is that Mary means "beloved of God." It is from two words, one Egyptian, "myr," which means beloved, the other Hebrew, "jam," which means God. The first woman in the Bible to be known as Mary was the sister of Moses and Aaron. These are both Egyptian names. Most probably their sister's name was also Egyptian, and in that language it means "beloved of God."

This explanation seems most correct when we consider that the Blessed Virgin was truly beloved of God. Of all men and women she was the only one who was always pleasing to God, because she alone was always free from sin, and hence always beloved of the Almighty. From all eternity God loved her. Out of love He created her; out of love He preserved her from sin; out of love He adorned her with every grace and beauty. In every sense her name is holy.

No wonder Mother Church honors her name. No wonder the saints and fathers of the Church have sung its praises. No wonder even those outside the fold have paid it tribute. No wonder the non-Catholic poet Longfellow penned this praise:

"Virgin and Mother of our dear Redeemer!
"All hearts are touched and softened at her name;

"Alike the bandit with the bloody hand,
"The priest, the prince, the scholar and the peasant,
"The man of deeds, the visionary dreamer,
"Pay homage to her as one ever present . . .
"And if our faith had given us nothing more
"Than this example of all womanhood,
"So mild, so merciful, so strong, so good,
"So patient, peaceful, loyal, loving, pure . . .
"This was enough to prove it higher and truer
"Than all the creeds the world has ever known."

Listen to St. Bonaventure:

"Blessed is the man who loves thy name, O Mary. Yes, truly blessed is he who loves thy sweet name, O Mother of God, for thy name is so glorious and admirable, that no one who remembers it has any fears at the hour of death."

"O salvation of all who invoke thee," he again exclaims, "I ask thee, O Mary, for the glory of thy name, to come and meet my soul when it is departing from this world, and to take it in thy arms . . . Be thou my soul's ladder and way to heaven."

And our own St. Anthony of Padua cried out: "O name of Mary! Joy in the heart, honey in the mouth, melody in the ear of her devout clients."

Would you have proof of what they declared? Then, dear friend, as you hear these praises, whisper quietly and lovingly: "Mary . . . Mary . . . Mary." Say it again and again, slowly, sweetly. Lift up your eyes and heart and voice to her. Repeat her name over and over: "Mary . . . Mary . . . Mary."

Especially when you call out to her, "Hail, Mary," remember the meaning of that title, "Beloved of God." Then you will know why the Introit of her feast begins with the sentence:

"My heart hath uttered a good word." Psalm 44.

Pray with Mother Church on that day:

"To Thy faithful people, rejoicing in the name and protection of the most holy Virgin Mary, vouchsafe, O Almighty God, we beseech Thee, through her loving intercession, to be delivered from all evils here on earth, and to be accounted worthy to enter everlasting joys in heaven."

Should you be privileged like the young lady of our story, should you be one of the countless many who were called after Mary in Baptism, should you be a religious who has added, as most women religious do, the name of Mary to your religious name—the Protestant poet Oliver Wendel Holmes is speaking to you. Nay, he is speaking to all of us who love her holy name:

"Is thy name Mary, maiden fair?
"Such should, methinks, its music be.
"The sweetest name that mortals bear,
"Were best befitting thee.
"And she to whom it once was given
"Was half of earth and half of heaven." Amen.

73

SEVEN DOLORS—September 15

"O all ye that pass by the way, attend and see if there be any sorrow like to my sorrow." Lam. 1:12.

In 1836 a man by the name of Siegfried Koehler left his native Alsace to find a new home in the new world. With him on the boat was a statue of the Sorrowful Mother which had been saved from a church threatened with destruction by the French Revolutionaries. A stormy sea almost sank their vessel. Siegfried brought his statue from the hold and led the crew and passengers in reciting the Litany of the Blessed Virgin Mary. To their prayers these pious Catholics added the promise to build a fitting shrine for Our Lady of Sorrows in the new world.

The prayer was heard. The promise, kept. At first it was only a little log hut. Later, by dint of begging through the countryside Siegfried was able to erect a brick shrine, which was completed and dedicated solemnly in 1871.

The shrine still stands just a few miles from Oldenburg, Indiana, the home of Holy Family Monastery, where reside the students of theology of the Franciscan Province of St. John the Baptist, which has headquarters in Cincinnati, Ohio.

Siegfried's ambition was to see Holy Mass celebrated at the shrine, but he did not live to see that desire fulfilled. He passed away kneeling beside his woodpile, saying the evening Angelus. Bishop Chartrand indulgenced prayers and visits at the shrine. In recent years the Sunday falling closest to the feast of the Seven Sorrows, September 15, has been set aside for the annual pilgrimage. It is a calm and quiet spot where nature helps the children of Mary think of her sorrows and pray to her.

Our Lady of Sorrows helped and blessed Siegfried and his immigrant family and friends. She will help everyone who sympathizes with her in her sadness. Mary had many mournful moments, but there were seven particularly sad incidents in her life. They were like seven swords piercing her innocent heart.

1. Forty days after Christ's birth Mary presented Him in the temple. The aged Simon, a just and devout servant of the Lord, took Jesus into his arms, and, inspired by the Holy Spirit, exclaimed:

"Behold, this child is destined for the fall and for the rise of many in Israel, and for a sign that shall be contradicted. And thy own soul a sword shall pierce, that the thoughts of many hearts may be revealed." St. Luke, 2:34.

Henceforth Mary's heart was filled with dread of the dire things predicted for her dear Son.

2. No sooner did the heartless Herod hear that Jesus, the infant King of the Jews, had been born, than he sought His life. But an angel of the Lord appeared to St. Joseph in a dream and warned:

"Arise, and take the child and his mother, and flee into Egypt, and remain there until I tell thee." St. Matthew, 1:13.

74

At once the Holy Family starts out for a strange land, where tradition tells us they remained for seven years, How painful and perilous that journey must have been. What anxiety and loneliness in a foreign country among unfriendly people. Oh, how Mary must have suffered on this trip and in this exile.

3. The third sword that pierced Our Lady's heart was the three day loss in the temple. At the age of twelve Jesus went with Mary and Joseph to Jerusalem. Only when they were returning did Mary and Joseph realize that Jesus was not with them. They hurried back and for three days sought him among friends and relatives. Finally they found Him in the temple, listening to the teachers there and asking them questions.

Some of the fathers say this was one of the bitterest sorrows for Mary because in her other trials and griefs she at least had Jesus with her, but now she was separated from Him and knew not where He was. Added to this was the fear that she was at fault or that Jesus had intentionally withdrawn from her life.

4. Her fourth great sorrow we remember in the fourth station of the Way of the Cross. Mary meets Jesus carrying His cross to Calvary. What a mournful meeting. Imagine the pain in Mary's heart to behold her Jesus groaning and staggering under the cruel cross. What anguish to see the One she loved so dearly being tortured by the taunts of the crowd as well as the weight of the wicked wood. And all the while she is prevented from helping Him.

5. But the sword will plunge still deeper. She must see Him shamefully stripped of His garments, rudely thrown upon the cross, and then hear the sickening strokes of the hammer. Helplessly and heart-broken she must stand beneath His death-bed, watching Him writhe in torture, listening to His parting words, listening for His parting breath.

6. And now comes the moment when they take Him from the cross. As each nail and each thorn was pulled from His body, it was a new blow to the heart of His Mother. How she must have hugged Him to her heart. How she must have tried to kiss Him back to life.

7. The seventh sword was to witness that broken, bloody body laid in the tomb. It was a Mother putting her Child to bed. What a grief-stricken good-night that was. Mary must have wished that she could bury her heavy heart with His.

As we recall these seven principal sorrows of Our Lady, be sure we are doing nothing morbid or pessimistic. We are recalling the griefs our good Mother went through for us. We are extending our sympathy to her. We are finding in these mournful moments of Mary's life consolation and inspiration for our own.

Mary appreciates our sympathy. She showed how grateful she is by helping the man of our story, Siegfried Koehler. She has shown her gratitude to millions of others who have grieved with and for her. May the feast of the Seven Dolors help us realize her part in the sufferings of Christ. Amen.

OUR LADY OF RANSOM—September 24

"If I have found favor in thy sight, O king, and if it please thee, give me my life for which I ask, and my people for which I request." Esther, 7:3.

Would you risk your life to free someone from a concentration camp? Would you take the place of a prisoner? Would you sacrifice comforts and even necessities to save a slave? Would you pray and do penance for the freedom of Christian captives?

These things were done by the followers of Christ from the earliest days, but especially during the Middle ages. At that time the enemies of Christ's Church had conquered a great part of Christian territory and had carried off into slavery many thousands of Christians. Hit and miss, though heroic, efforts to free these unfortunates had been made here and there.

The Church decided to organize the work of ransoming slaves. In 1198 St. John of Matha and St. Felix of Valois founded the Trinitarians. From then until 1787 they redeemed 900,000 captives. The Order of Our Lady of Ransom, called the Mercedarians, and founded by St. Peter Nolasco, ransomed 490,736 slaves between the years 1218 and 1632. St. Vincent de Paul, a slave himself, led his priests to save 1200 Christian captives in the short period between 1642 and 1660 at the staggering cost of 1,200,000 pounds of silver. An even greater achievement was the conversion of thousands in captivity, and steeling them against the sufferings of a cruel martyrdom for the faith.

All this has been admitted by a modern, competent Protestant historian, Bonet-Maury. He records that no expedition sent into the Barbary States by the powers of Europe or America equalled "the moral effect produced by the ministry of consolation, peace and abnegation, going even to the sacrifice of liberty and life, which was exercised by the humble sons of St. John of Matha, St. Peter Nolasco, and St. Vincent de Paul."

It is a far cry from the 1200's to the 1900's. It is a far cry from Portugal and Spain of that day to Russia and her captive neighbors of today. However, in scarcely any other instance has history so exactly repeated itself. As you read these lines millions of Christians, Catholics for the most part, are starving and dying in slavery. Only the recording angel can count the millions in Red concentration camps at this moment, the millions doing slave labor in foreign lands, the added millions cowering under the Russian sickle, as thousands cowered centuries ago under the Moorish crescent.

Who can count the displaced persons, driven from their homes and native lands, roaming the roads of the world without food, without shelter, without clothing? Who is responsible for this mass slavery? The enemies of Christ, principally the rulers of Russia.

That is why the Feast of Our Lady of Ransom, September 24, is particularly important. Our Blessed Mother herself appeared in vision to St. Peter Nolasco, and requested him to found a religious order devoted to the rescue of captives. This was in 1218.

Previous to that, since 1192, certain noblemen of Barcelona, Spain, had organized to care for the sick in hospitals and to rescue Christians from the Moors. St. Peter Nolasco, St. Raymond of Pennafort, and King James formed the new Order of Our Lady of Mercy. The group included religious priests who prayed and gathered the means, while the lay monks or knights went into the very camps of the Moors to buy back Christians, and, if necessary, take their very places. We have mentioned the magnitude of their success, a success that was won through the heavenly assistance of the Mother of Mercy, Our Lady of Ransom.

We cannot take the places of the 20 million Russians enslaved in their own land. We cannot buy freedom for the 2 million Germans doing slave labor in Russia. We cannot substitute for the slaves in Red-dominated regions of Europe. But we can and must beseech Our Lady of Ransom to show her powerful concern toward these miserable millions. We can beg her to help them find their way home. We can pray her powerful intercession that slavery of all kinds may disappear from the earth. There is also a slavery of sin, from which she is eager to deliver us and our loved ones and all the world.

Put yourself in the position of these displaced unfortunates. Imagine yourself exiled to a strange land, with strange customs, a strange language, and a merciless master. Picture yourself without a home, without friends, and often without your family.

Let your representative in congress know that no political pebble may be left unturned in the effort to help and free our fellow citizens held in bondage throughout the world.

Above all let your heavenly representative and advocate, Our Lady of Ransom, know that you are interested, you are concerned, you are begging her help for these unfortunates.

Best of all, attend Mass and receive Holy Communion and pray with the Church on this ever-timely feast:

"O God, who by means of the most glorious Mother O Thy Son was pleased to give new children to Thy Church for the deliverance of Christ's faithful from the power of the heathen; grant, we beseech Thee, that we who love and honor her as the foundress of so great a work may, by her merits and intercession, be ourselves delivered from all sin and from the bondage of the evil one. Through the same Christ, our Lord, Amen."

HOLY ROSARY—October 7

"Who shall find a valiant woman? far and from the uttermost coasts is the price of her." Proverbs, 31:10.

Some years ago the news of a terrible disaster at sea shocked the nation. The steamer Morro Castle caught fire off the Atlantic coast, sending scores to death by fire and water. Among those saved was a young Catholic lady, Marion Slack by name. Hearing the cry, "Fire! Fire," seeing frantic dashes for lifebelts and lifeboats, she realized that she had to swim or burn.

Digging her Rosary from her purse, she knelt down on the deck, breathed a few Hail Mary's, and then with her beads clutched tightly in her hand, she leaped into the ocean. For seven agonizing hours she managed to keep afloat, until another ship fished her out of the raging waters. Exhausted as she was, she still clasped firmly in her hand what was left of her Rosary. Many of the beads had been crushed and had slipped through her fingers. The cross was imbedded in the flesh of her hand. When she was able to talk the young lady exclaimed:

"I would have given up; I would have quit, if it had not been for my trust in the Rosary. I just knew that the Blessed Mother would help me."

Life is like that. Life is a sea, for many a stormy sea. We have all we can do to keep our heads above water, physically, financially, spiritually. We are washed about by almost over-whelming waves of illness, temptation, disappointment, set-backs and the sucking undertow of discouragement. We want to give up; to cease swimming, to stop striving; to go under. We simply can't make it.

In our struggle we are not alone. There is someone who can and will help us; someone who hovers above the sea of life; someone who is all-powerful at the throne of God; someone to whom we appeal, as did that brave young lady, through the Rosary. That someone is the Blessed Virgin Mother of God, the Star of life's sea.

The Catholic Church considers the beads so important, so valuable, so helpful that she sets aside a special feast of the Holy Rosary, October 7, and that entire month as a time to pay special attention to praying the Rosary, a time to renew and increase our devotion to this favorite prayer of Our Lady.

You have no time? You have as much time as a prominent and busy New York lawyer, who declared: "I have a tiny Rosary which fits snugly in my hand and it is my greatest help amid the hustle and bustle of the business world. Every morning on my way to the office or court I say my beads, and among the thousands who brush elbows with me not one knows that I am talking to the Mother of God."

Take time for at least a decade in the morning and another in the evening, or on your way to and from work. Say it with your family right after the evening meal. Put a little trust in Mary's Rosary. Like that girl who kept on struggling because she trusted and hoped in Mary, we too must keep on struggling against the waves of misfortune, sickness, poverty, and the whisperings of "Danny Demon"—but always Rosary in hand.

"Hear, sweet Mother, hear the weary,
"Tossed upon life's troubled sea;
"Gentle, guiding Star of ocean,
"Lead thy children home to thee."

And this sweet Mother's ear is bent deepest to hear you during Holy Mass. Some have said that the Rosary is not an ideal Mass prayer. But I have seen many kneeling before the altar, clinging to their Rosary as hopefully and helplessly as the young lady struggling in the swirling sea, for example, those with poor eyesight, the hard of hearing, the shaky, the myopic, the nervous, the illiterate, and even those who can see and read and understand, but who want to be unencumbered with a book though still clinging to something.

There is a close connection between the Sublime Sacrifice and this garland of roses. The sign of the cross, the theme of the Mass, is the theme song of the Rosary. The tribute to the Trinity can be turned to a tribute to the Trinity in the Creed on the altar. "Born of the Virgin Mary," is echoed in "born again upon the altar." The Our Father is in thought and word a part of Mass. The greeting of the angel and the Incarnation finds renewal on the snow-white linens. The Glory be is the be-all and end-all of what takes place on the Calvary of your church.

The mysteries remind us of the realities taking place before us. The hope-inspiring Incarnation, the quiet Visitation, the still and solemn Birth —of these the Mass reminds us. The Crowning, the Scourging, the Way to Calvary, the Death—what are these but the essence of Mass? And the ecstasy of the simplest low Mass, to say nothing of the tingling uplift of a solemn Sacrifice, is but the acting out of the glorious mysteries. It stands to reason that an act of homage to the Mother simply has to be in some close way connected with the Son. So take your Rosary to Mass, if you will. Take it everywhere with you.

As that young lady wrestled with almost overpowering waves of water, so must we come to grips with temptation, distraction, fatigue, illness, worry, and anxiety. No more than she can we swim through, unless we clutch closely and devotedly our Rosary.

It seems impossible that a weak, frail thing like a ring of roses can do such heavy duty in the stress of life. It seems slightly fragile as a life preserver. Will it really hold if I hang on to it? Will it buoy me up? Will it support me above the waves? Will the Rosary give me, as it gave that girl, the strength and courage to keep on trying?

The Rosary will do that and more. Try it. Amen.

MATERNITY OF OUR LADY—October 12

"The Holy One to be born shall be called the Son of God." St. Luke, 1:35.

The following incident took place on March 4, 1881. A new president of the United States had been elected. He lived near Cleveland, Ohio. A few days before he was to take office he wrote to his old mother:

"I want you to go to Washington with me."

The mother was surprised and after thinking it over she wrote to tell him how proud she was. But she added:

"I cannot go to Washington. I would be quite out of place there among the great people whom you will meet. I'll stay at home and pray for you."

Quickly came her son's answer:

"I'll not go without you."

As a result, mother and son traveled together to the capitol city. They stayed at the same hotel and when the time for the ceremony came, together they left the hotel, together they entered the carriage, and together they drove to the capitol, where the great crowd of over 100,000 was waiting.

It was a great occasion. The high platform was occupied by all the celebrated men of the country, by governors, judges, foreign ministers and government officials. Before the platform was a great sea of faces, all turned up to the person who was to become the president of the United States. Everyone noticed that, instead of taking the chair provided for him, the president-to-be offered it to his mother. He then delivered his inaugural address, and after he had taken the oath of office, he walked over, put his arms around his mother, and kissed her. The great crowd was thrilled at this devotion of a son to a mother.

That president was James A. Garfield, who was later martyred. He had done one of the most beautiful things in his life. Everyone went home admiring his desire to honor his mother along with himself, to share his honors with his own mother. Certainly nobody in that vast assemblage felt that these marks of love took away a bit of the power and prestige of the presidency.

Why wonder then that the Son of God honored His Mother, and wants us to honor her? As we approach the feast of the Maternity of Our Lady on October 12, we would like to consider three things:

1. Mary is truly the Mother of God.

2. As the Mother of God Mary claims the greatest dignity next to God.

3. As Mother of God we must honor and venerate her above all other creatures in heaven and on earth.

1. The greatest joy of a mother is to see her son honored and respected. It is a great joy for a mother to say of a good man: "This is my son."

Mary experienced that joy. She knew that Jesus was God. I would suggest that every one of you read the story in St. Luke, 1:26-35, of the announcement by the Angel Gabriel to Mary that she was to be the Mother of God. Especially let me quote for you the concluding words of the angel:

"The Holy Ghost shall come upon thee, and the power of the Most High shall overshadow thee. And therefore the Holy One to be born shall be called the Son of God."

The Son of Mary is called the Son of the Most High, the Son of God. As soon as Mary gave her consent, the Second Person of the Blessed Trinity took a body and soul in her most chaste womb. From the very first instant of their existence the body and soul of Christ were united to His Divinity.

Christ, remember, had two natures, the divine and the human. But Christ was only one Person, the divine, and this Divine Person was true Man while He remained true God.

It is this fact and this glorious truth we celebrate on October 12, the feast of the Maternity of Our Lady. Mary did not give to Christ His Divine Being. She gave to Him His human nature. But that human nature was intimately united with His divine nature. Therefore Mary can be called and is the Mother of God.

This title had been foretold long before. We quote Isaias:

"Behold a virgin shall be with child, and bring forth a son, and they shall call his name Emmanuel, which being interpreted, is God with us." Isaias, 7:14.

Elizabeth was inspired to exclaim:

"Whence is this to me that the mother of my Lord should come to me?" St. Luke, 1:43.

Mother Church, the infallible teacher of God's truth, has expressly declared that Mary is the Mother of God.

2. As Mother of God Mary enjoys the greatest dignity next to that of God Himself. A creature becomes the Mother of the Creator. A weak, helpless maiden becomes the Mother of the Allpowerful and Eternal God. All the titles of earth fade in importance when compared with the title, "Mother of God." We might recall our story of President Garfield inviting his mother to the platform at his inauguration. The mother of the president— what an honor that was. No other mother in the whole United States could compare in dignity with the mother of the president. So too Christ wants His Mother honored as Mother of God, Mother of Jesus who was both God and Man.

3. Because Mary is the Mother of God, because she enjoys a place next to God Himself, because she enjoys such a high dignity, it is only reasonable that we should honor and venerate her above all creatures. We Catholics do not adore or worship her. We adore God alone. However, we do honor her, we do respect her, we do venerate the Mother of Jesus, just as any other son, like President Garfield, would honor his mother and hope that others would honor her.

The attention we give to Mary does not take away from the worship of her Son. On the contrary, it increases the devotion to her Child. May Mary lead us and the whole world to the heart of her Son. Amen.

OUR LADY OF FATIMA—October 13

"And nothing will be impossible to you. But this kind can only be cast out by prayer and fasting." St. Matthew, 17:20.

Our Lady of Fatima has gone even into prison cells. A prisoner in London was awaiting trial. He picked up a copy of the *London Universe,* an excellent Catholic paper. His attention was drawn to the story of a pilgrimage to a shrine of Our Lady of Fatima in Bala, North Wales. He wrote to the organizer, a Mrs. McGrath, asking her to send him the paper regularly.

The man was convicted, but while serving his sentence he was received into the Third Order of St. Francis. He persuaded fourteen other jailmates to attend daily Mass with him and recite the Rosary. A statue of Our Lady of Fatima was purchased by Mrs. McGrath and placed in a small niche before the prisoner's heavily barred cell window. It is a constant inspiration to prayer and penance for the prisoners.

What is the story behind this devotion which is sweeping the world, even going behind bars? In 1917, near the village of Fatima in Portugal, the Blessed Virgin appeared six times to three little shepherd children. Jacinta was seven years of age, Francis was nine, and Lucy was ten. Mary told this trio that God wanted to establish throughout the world devotion to her Immaculate Heart. She told them that men must stop offending her Divine Son, and that they should pray the Rosary in order to end the war which was then raging. This appearance took place at noon on May 13, 1917. Our Blessed Lady asked her young friends to come back to the same place on the 13th of each month for the next six months.

Despite opposition from parents and town authorities, the children came back each month except during August. Mary told them to say the Rosary every day and spend some time thinking about the eternal mysteries, instead of merely mumbling prayers. She asked that people go to Confession and Communion on the first Saturday of five consecutive months. If this were done Mary promised to help at the hour of death with the graces needed for salvation.

Our Blessed Lady also uttered a solemn warning that, if her requests were not heeded, another terrible war would break out, different nations would be destroyed, famine and persecution would reign, many would be martyred, and the Holy Father would suffer much.

On the other hand, if the faithful heeded her warnings and mended their lives and were devoted to her Immaculate Heart, even Russia would be converted and there would be world peace.

In October of 1917, 70,000 people gathered on the spot where Mary had appeared to these children. In honor of His Blessed Mother God worked a stupendous miracle, the so-called miracle of the sun. When the tremendous crowd gathered, the sun changed color from gold to silver. It sent in every direction rays of different colored lights. Three times for four minutes each time the sun moved around like a wheel of fire and then to the consternation of everyone it began tumbling down to the earth, coming so close that many thought the end of the world was at hand.

In the sky the children saw Our Lady with St. Joseph and the Divine Infant, who later blessed the crowd. Finally Mary appeared in the garb of Our Lady of Mount Carmel. At this time Mary announced simply and firmly:

"I am the Lady of the Rosary."

The face of Our Blessed Mother became very grave as she gave the children her last message:

"People must amend their lives, ask pardon for their sins and not offend our Lord any more, for He is already too much offended."

As she prepared to leave she opened her hands and from them rays of light stretched in the direction of the sun.

Is there any meaning in this story of Fatima for you and for me? What is that meaning? Clearly Mary has brought a message to the world, a message we might put into four points or requests:

1. Turn away from sin. Make any sacrifice to fulfill the duties of your state in life.

2. Consecrate yourself without reserve to the Immaculate Heart of Mary and live up to that consecration.

3. Recite the Rosary every day. After each decade add: "O, my Jesus, forgive our sins; save us from the fire of hell and lead all souls to heaven, especially those who have most need of your mercy."

4. Keep the five First Saturdays by receiving the sacraments, by reciting five decades of the Rosary and by meditating fifteen minutes on the fifteen mysteries of the Rosary.

This devotion is offered to the Immaculate Heart of Mary.

Suppose our Blessed Mother had appeared to you and told you what she told those three children. Suppose Mary would back up her words with a startling miracle. Surely you would listen. Surely you would try to carry out her requests, because we know she is interested in every one of us, she is interested in all the things of God, particularly in world peace.

Mary asks two things in particular: prayer and penance. This request reminds us of the incident when Jesus cast out evil spirits after His followers had failed to do so. When the disciples asked the reason for their failure Jesus told them that "this kind can only be cast out by prayer and fasting." St. Matthew, 17:20.

The devils of destruction are abroad in the world today, driving nations into war, destroying peace in the hearts of individuals and in the council chambers of nations. Only prayer and penance can win peace. Only prayer and penance can restore peace. Listen to the call of Our Lady of Fatima. On her feast day, October 13, tell her that you will heed her warning and follow her advice. Amen.

PURITY OF OUR LADY—October 16

"All the glory of the king's daughter is within in golden borders, clothed round about with varieties." Psalm 44:14.

One of the greatest religious books, next to the Bible, is *The Following of Christ.* Many say it was written by Thomas a Kempis, a very saintly soul. This servant of God tells of an experience he had in his struggle to remain pure.

One evening, after he had recited his prayers and retired, he was beset with the most frightful and horrible images, which finally awakened him. Even awake the powerful temptation continued. Thomas started to pray to the Blessed Virgin as was his practice in all temptation. He began to pray the Hail Mary. With his mind entirely on his prayer he began, "Hail Mary." But the temptation continued, even seemed to grow worse. But he went on, "Full of grace." The devil never desisted. "The Lord is with thee," prayed a Kempis. Still Satan tried to sway the saint. "Blessed art thou among women," he said with all the fervor in his soul. Nevertheless, there was no let-up by the evil one. Finally he came to the words, "And blessed is the fruit of thy womb, Jesus." With deeper reverence and determination he pronounced those words especially the holy name of Jesus. Suddenly his soul was at peace. The impure imaginations and suggestions vanished; Thomas experienced a holy peace and quiet of heart.

This incident, which could be multiplied by the hundreds of thousands in the history of Christianity, points to one of the reasons we honor the purity of Mary, namely, the help she gives to those who really want to be pure. Mother Church even sets aside a day on which we honor this fact, the feast of the Purity of Our Lady on October 16. It will be well for us to think of Mary's purity, at least from a few angles. We would like to point out at the time of this feast first, that the purity of Mary was of the highest order; second, that she preserved and kept her purity by penance and prayer; third, that Mary's purity has inspired countless souls with a love of this virtue.

1. The purity of Mary was most excellent. As a little child she was taught the importance of this virtue, and as the years went on kept herself pure. As a child she made a promise to Almighty God to remain a virgin, even though this was long before the time when virginity was considered something desirable. On the contrary, this promise of Mary is all the more excellent when we remember that before her time virginal purity was almost an unknown virtue. In fact, the women of the Old Testament considered childlessness as a curse.

Virginity, dedicating oneself to the Lord as a virgin, was not held in favor by the people of the Old Law. Every woman hoped that she might be the mother of the promised Redeemer. In face of all this tradition, Mary promised God always to remain a virgin. Mary was even willing to give up the honor of being the Mother of God in order to remain true to that promise, as we see in the incident when the angel told her of her high calling.

2. Mary preserved and promoted her purity by sacrifice and prayer. It is

true that in Mary's case the virtue of purity was the effect of God's grace. It is also true that she was free from all inclination and temptation to sin against this or any other virtue. Nevertheless, she used every means possible to remain pure and holy.

Her modesty she learned and developed living in the temple as a little girl. Every posture, every movement, the very tone of her voice, everything about her showed the desire of her mind and heart to be forever chaste. She watched her eyes. She mortified her ears by not listening to idle gossip, her tongue by not repeating the small bits of information that she might have heard from others. She mortified her hands by using them in the work of daily life. In addition to this exterior sacrifice she controlled her thoughts and imaginations.

Furthermore, Mary prayed to always remain pure. Her heart was always united to God in prayer. As a little one growing up in the temple, she learned to pray and loved to pray. How beautiful and sweet those prayers must have been in the sight of God.

3. The purity of Mary has inspired countless souls with a love of this angelic virtue. Her example has been the greatest power in the world for pure and holy people. It has produced abundant fruits. Look at St. Joseph, her holy spouse. From Mary he learned to know and love holy purity. Look at St. John who was chosen to care for the Mother of Jesus because of his purity. In the first centuries thousands braved wild beasts and death rather than sacrifice this virtue. The story of Christianity is studded with saintly souls who found in Mary the model and also the help to purity. The story from the life of Thomas a Kempis is repeated in the lives of St. Benedict, St. Bernard, St. Thomas Aquinas, St. Casimir and St. Francis de Sales.

As we approach the feast of the Purity of Our Lady, October 16, remember how wonderful her purity was, how spotless, how snow-white, how absolutely without blemish. Remember how Mary preserved this angelic virtue by penance and by prayer. Recall how the saints and holy people of all walks of life and all ages kept this virtue with the thought of Mary in mind and with the grace of Mary in their hearts.

Keep these thoughts before you always and the angelic power of purity will be more easy for you to keep, easier to acquire, and easier to recover if it has been lost. Our Lady of the pure will help you. Amen.

OUR LADY OF SUFFRAGE—(Week day in the Octave of All Saints)

"What wilt thou, Queen Esther, what is thy request? If thou shouldst ask even one half of the kingdom, it shall be given to thee." Esther, 5:1.

A non-Catholic woman from Australia was making a tour of England. She visited Westminster Abbey, taking a seat near the beautiful statue of Mary in Our Lady's Chapel. There in quiet thought she took in the meaning of the beautiful statuary and decorations. Presently she saw two poorly clad, ragged little children enter the cathedral and toddle up the aisle. One was about eight years old, the other about four. They walked hand in hand up to the statue of Our Lady. Down they knelt at her shrine. From the expression on their faces one could see they were praying earnestly. Evidently they were asking something important from our Blessed Mother.

The Australian lady watched them go out together. The thought came to her that perhaps there is something these children needed. She hurried after the little ones and asked if they were asking for something special.

"Yes," the older replied, "mother sent us to ask the Blessed Virgin to give us shoes. Father is out of work and cannot buy us any."

The visitor opened her purse and gave the children all the money she had with her. Their little faces were happy. The Mother of God had heard their appeal.

In countless cases the Mother of God has heard the appeal of those who have come to her with trust and confidence. We call Mary our Advocate, the one who intercedes for us. At this season we celebrate the feast of Our Lady of Suffrage. Suffrage means an intercessory prayer, that is, a prayer by someone who is a sort of go-between. Intercession means that someone asks or prays for somebody else. Our Lady of Suffrage means that Mary offers our prayers for us. We want to consider how Mary is our go-between.

1. Mary is our merciful Advocate. Just as Queen Esther in the Old Testament appealed for the people of her own race, those who were near and dear to her, and received from the king the promise that he would give her whatever she asked even if it would be half of the kingdom, so Mary seated beside the King of heaven receives a promise, as it were, from Almighty God that He will grant to her whatever she asks. Out of mercy Queen Esther interceded for her Jewish people, and her prayer was heard. Out of mercy Mary intercedes for her sons and daughters on earth, and God hears her prayer. Mary always felt merciful toward the human race. As a little girl she heard the story of man's beginning, of the creation of Adam and Eve, of their fall, and of the promise that a Redeemer would come to save the world. In her heart was the longing that she might at least be a servant girl in the house of the Lord. When she was chosen to be the Mother of the Messias her heart was filled with pity toward all.

In every age and in every place she has listened to the sighs and groans of those who were in distress of soul or body. From the high court of heaven she looks down with eyes of mercy upon our miseries. Not one of our pains misses her motherly eye. Often the world fails to see hidden anguish in hearts and homes. Often our fellow men cannot see or sympathize with the burdens that oppress our souls. But Mary sees them all and feels merciful toward all. That is why we call her Our Lady of Suffrage.

2. **Mary is a powerful Advocate with Almighty God.** In the Old Testament Moses, by holding up his hands in prayer, was able to stay the wrath of God against a sinful people. If God heard the prayer of Moses, how much more readily will He hear the prayer of His own mother. Furthermore, Mary is dear to Almighty God on many scores. She was the Mother of God's Son. When the person who asks something is dear to the one who is asked, the petitioner will be more likely to receive his or her request. In this case, the intercessor, our Blessed Mother, is dear to Almighty God. Hence her intercession is powerful.

Again, prayer is powerful when it is offered by one who has some right to plead a certain cause. Mary has the right to plead for us because she is our Mother. Jesus gave us to her and gave her to us.

3. **Mary is an effective Advocate.** By that we mean whatever she asks for she obtains. Of course she leaves it up to the Lord, but God knows that Mary will ask for nothing except what is in harmony with His Divine Will. We see Mary's effective help in the lives of the saints. We see it in the life of everyone who appeals to her sincerely and perseveringly. Every individual, every community, every country that has ever asked her intercession, has experienced her help. Only the book of the recording angel will tell us how many plagues and famines and earthquakes and fires and floods and other calamities of soul and body have been averted through prayer to Mary.

Each one of us has experienced her suffrage, her intercession. Often you have heard a mother tell a child after it is grown up of the many dangers and scrapes from which mother rescued the little one when it could not help itself. So, too, the children of Mary do not realize at the time, cannot realize how many dangers she has kept from us. Every single one of us can repeat the words of St. Augustine to our Blessed Mother:

"I have offended thee and thou hast defended me."

When we realize how good Mary has been to us and to the world, when we realize that she is a merciful, powerful and effective advocate at the throne of God, we will pledge anew our loyalty to her. Especially on the feast of Our Lady of Suffrage we will tell her of our trust and confidence. Amen.

PATRONAGE OF OUR LADY
(During week before second Sunday of November)

"The Lord hath blessed thee by his power, because by thee he hath brought our enemies to naught." Judith, 13:22.

In the ages of faith there stood at almost every street corner of Paris a little shrine raised a few feet above street level. Each contained a small, rudely carved image of the Madonna. Often the image was black with age. Sometimes it was covered with lace and with flowers in season.

In every one of those shrines tiny lamps were lit. Like stars they glowed all through the night and all day Saturday. At the first peep of dawn people would make their way to these spots to say their morning prayers. This was the first beginning of lighting streets, an essential thing in modern life. Those lamps told the passerby that someone was watching, someone was on guard, someone who was interested and powerful to protect, our Blessed Mother.

This pious practice comes to mind as we approach the feast of the Patronage of Our Lady which is celebrated during the week before the second Sunday of November. This feast is not kept universally at present. It goes back to 1679. On May 6 of that year the Sacred Congregation of Rites gave permission for all the provinces of Spain to celebrate this feast in memory of and in thanksgiving for the victories over the Moors and other enemies of Spain. Benedict XII ordered this feast kept in the Papal States on the third Sunday of November. In other places this feast is kept on some Sunday in November set aside by the ordinary of the diocese. The office for the day is the common one of the Blessed Virgin and the Mass begins with the words, "Hail, Holy Mother."

Patronage means the office, the function or status of a patron. A patron is one who has been chosen or named, one who is honored as a special guardian, as a particular protector or supporter of some group or community or nation. In that sense Mary is the patroness of the entire Catholic Church, because she is the special guardian, the special protector, the special spiritual supporter of the children of the Church.

Of course she was the particular patroness of the French people in the days when they were still loyal to Almighty God, just as Mary is at present the principal patroness of many other nations, notably the United States. On this feast of the Patronage of Our Lady we might consider a few ways in which Mary is our protector and our guardian: Mary protects her devout children during life; she protects them at the hour of death; she helps her children even after death.

1. The protection of Mary through life is something we have seen in the history of nations and the lives of individuals. Mary helps in every kind of physical difficulty. She saves from robbery and murder, from flood and fire, from death in battle and on the highway.

But the protection Mary gives our bodies is not nearly as important as that which she gives to our souls. Constantly the devil is seeking to snare souls. Constantly Mary opposes him. Many saints were tempted by the world, the flesh, and the devil. St. Louis, King of France, was repeatedly tempted to vanity. St. Stanislaus Kostka was tempted to give up his vocation. But these and countless other heroes and heroines of God hastened to the heart of Mary and there found the help they needed to keep their souls in the grace of God.

2. Mary protects her clients at the hour of death. At that time the devil makes a supreme effort to win the soul away from God. And it is at that moment when Mary is nearest, when she is beside every one of her sons and daughters. That protection at that hour we can expect because thousands of times during life we have prayed to her:

"Holy Mary, Mother of God, pray for us sinners now and at the hour of our death."

Mary strengthens our souls that we will not despair, that we will not give in to discouragement and despondency. Her protection at the hour of death is also given to our bodies. Sorrows and sufferings come at that instant. For many they are painful and dreadful. Mary is there to soothe the feverish brow, to encourage the troubled heart, to inspire the departing soul. Mary has even appeared to some of her children at that hour, notably St. Bernard, St. Francis Regis, St. Philip Neri, and others.

Show her your love during life and she will be with you in death. Show your devotion to her by joining her societies or sodalities, by wearing her scapular or medal, by visiting her altars and shrines, by reciting her litany and other prayers, particularly by praying her Rosary. The best devotion is imitating her virtues. All such devotion is difficult at times, but it wins her motherly love and attention.

3. Mary is our patron not only during life and at the hour of death, but also after death. Too many Catholics have the mistaken idea that all will be well if they manage to stay out of hell. They say:

"I'll be satisfied to get to purgatory."

Such people forget that the pains of purgatory are greater than any on this earth. Like a true mother, Mary nevertheless will help the suffering soul that was devoted to her. She told St. Bridget of Sweden: "I am the compassionate advocate of my devoted client not only in this life but still more in the life to come."

Mary helps departed souls by inspiring relatives, friends and others to pray for them. Mary helps suffering souls by applying to them the prayers and penances and good deeds of all her devoted children. She helps immeasurably by her own merits and prayers.

Where could you find a more interested patron, a more powerful and merciful protector? May Mary show her patronage to every one of us—during life, at death, and after death. Amen.

MOTHER OF DIVINE PROVIDENCE
(Saturday before the third Sunday of November)

"Cast thy care upon the Lord, and He shall sustain thee." Psalm 54:23.

Father Beauregard was a famous preacher of the last century. After delivering his famous sermon on divine providence a visitor stopped to tell him:

"Father, I heard your sermon. You spoke well, but I am come to tell you that I am living proof of the contrary of what you said. There is no providence for me."

"How, sir, what words are these to speak?"

"Well, Father," the man went on, "you may judge for yourself. I am a carpenter. I have a wife and three children. We all work hard. We have never harmed anyone. For twenty years I have been trying to serve the Lord and live as a good Christian. I have always put my trust in God, hoping that He would come to my assistance. But all in vain. I am ready to throw myself in the river for I have bills coming due the 30th of this month which I am entirely unable to meet. I am lost, dishonored, and I would rather die than live."

"Well, my dear friend," said Father, "you shall yourself become a sensible monument of Divine Providence. How much money do you need?"

"Ah, Father, how good you are. With less than 3000 francs I am saved."

"My friend," said Father, "there are 2,500 francs. I could not give it to you myself, but some days ago the Princess di Conti, after hearing my sermon on alms, sent me that money authorizing me to use it in whatever way I thought proper for the unfortunate. Go, meet your engagements and never again say that there is no providence."

In this story we see one of the ways in which Divine Providence works, how God uses His own creatures to show that He is taking care of us. In this case He used Princess di Conti, a woman of wealth, and a Catholic priest as an intermediary, to help the head of a family to meet his obligations.

In this Princess we see a figure of Our Blessed Lady whom we honor during November with the feast, Mother of Divine Providence. Mary was closely associated with Divine Providence throughout her life, and continues to cooperate with an all-provident Father from her throne in heaven. Providence means the attention and desire of God to preserve the physical and moral order which He has established in creation. Providence includes infinite wisdom, that is, a knowledge of all creatures and their needs. It includes infinite goodness, that is, the desire of God to choose the best means to supply those needs. It includes infinite power, namely, the ability to meet those needs. Divine Providence shows itself:

1. In bestowing on creatures whatever is necessary and helpful to their good and happiness. The slightest study of nature proves that someone is guiding and providing. The clothing of animals, the migration of birds, and the adaptation of flowers show an all-wise Providence.

2. Providence shows itself in preserving creatures from evils which are opposed to their true ends.

3. Providence shows itself in guiding creatures to their particular purpose for which they were made. We see this in the study of nature and in the story of man.

4. How do we know there is a Providence in the physical order?

A. We know it from Sacred Scripture which tells us time and again that God takes care of His creatures.

B. All nations have recognized that there is a supreme Wisdom overseeing and guiding all things.

C. The happenings in nature show that there are certain laws governing all things made. Laws require a Law-giver.

5. We know that there is a Providence in the moral order also, namely, in the matter of right and wrong.

A. God Himself has said that He is interested in what we do. In fact, the Son of God taught us to call Almighty God, "Our Father."

B. The story of nations shows that man lives under the government of God, that God is pleased when we obey Him, and displeased when we disobey Him.

C. If God takes care of the physical order it stands to reason that He certainly will take care also of the more important matters of the spirit.

In all this care for His creatures God uses other creatures, principally His own Mother Mary whom we honor and greet as Mother of Divine Providence. Let us look at some of the reasons for that title:

1. Mary knew the plan of God and entered into the spirit of that arrangement.

2. Mary heard Jesus tell about the lilies of the field and the sparrows and how God takes care of them.

3. Mary saw Jesus put aside some of the laws of creation to work miracles of all kinds. She even asked Him to work His first public miracle.

4. Mary stood beneath the cross where Divine Providence went to the limit in taking care of the souls of men.

5. Mary was present at the founding of the infant Church. She inspired and encouraged the Apostles.

6. Ever since Mary has been interested in the Church of her Son. Like the Princess of our story, Mary has been entrusted with a wealth of grace which she dispenses freely, generously, either personally or through others.

7. If her own Son would die for you, then surely Mary is interested enough to help you in whatever way she can. Truly she is the Mother of Divine Providence.

In troubled times like ours it is good, it is necessary to remember that God is still watching over us and that the Mother of God, the Mother of Divine Providence, like a true mother, is also watching over us.

As the Psalm tells us: "Cast thy care upon the Lord and He shall sustain thee." We might also say: "Cast your care upon the Mother of the Lord and she will sustain and provide for thee." Amen.

91

PRESENTATION—November 21

"O thou most beautiful among women." Canticles 5:9.

Do you ever read seed catalogues, especially the announcements of flower growers? Ordinarily I don't either, because I do not have the gift of the "green thumb," the talent of a good gardener. However, while giving a mission for a priest who was quite a flower fancier, I learned a little about the care of flowers in their early stages.

On the floor of the clothes closet in the guest room assigned to me were several glass jars with some fairly good-sized bulbs in each. In a light vein I asked the pastor if he was raising onions. He showed me the catalogue from which he had ordered the bulbs. There I read the directions for their care:

"Keep them," said the book, "in a dark room where there is just enough warmth to start them growing slowly. This will cause the bulbs to throw out roots while the leaves remain at comparative rest. This is very important. If exposed to light and too much heat, the leaves will be stirred to sprout rapidly, while the roots have not yet had a chance to reach and spread out to insure a sufficient supply of nourishment. Result: a weak and imperfect flowering. Let the roots spread and grow first. Then gradually increase the light and heat, and you will have flowers like those illustrated above."

Whether the good father ever reaped such rosy results, I did not make it a point to find out, but often since the thought has occurred that here was an illustration from nature of the importance of the hidden life as a preparation for public work. It is an apt illustration of the girlhood of the Mother of God. In this case the Father of all reared the most beautiful Flower that ever grew.

Of Mary's hidden life Scripture tells us nothing. Of her presentation in the temple, which we celebrate November 21, the inspired writings give no word. Nevertheless, we do have the testimony of tradition, which in turn is based on accounts from apostolic times. For instance, in the Proto-evangelium of St. James, which is apocryphal, we read:

"And the child was two years old, and Joachim said: 'Let us take her up to the temple of the Lord, that we may pay the vow which we have vowed, lest perchance the Lord send to us, and our offering be not received.' And Anna said: 'Let us wait for the third year, in order that the child may not seek for father and mother.' And Joachim said: 'Invite the daughters of the Hebrews that are undefiled, and let them take each a lamp, and let them stand with the lamps burning, that the child may not turn back, and her heart be captivated from the temple of the Lord.' And the priest received her, and kissed her, and blessed her, saying: 'The Lord has magnified thy name in all generations. In thee, on the last of the days, the Lord will manifest His redemption to the sons of Israel.' And he set her down upon the third step of the altar, and the Lord God sent grace upon her; and she danced with her feet, and all the house of Israel loved her."

Another book called *The Nativity of Mary* adds this note:

"But the parents having offered up their sacrifice, according to the custom of the law, and perfected their vow, left the Virgin with the other virgins in the apartments of the temple, who were to be brought up there, and they returned home."

St. John of Damascus expresses the belief of the early Christians in a way that brings out our thought of Mary's hidden life being like that of a plant or flower being nurtured for better things:

"The Holy Virgin first saw the light in Joachim's house hard by the Probatica and was brought to the temple. There, having been planted in the House of God, and nourished by the Spirit, like a fruitful olive tree, she became the home of every virtue, turning her mind away from every carnal and secular desire, and thus keeping her soul as well as her body virginal, as was meet for her who was to receive God into her bosom: for as He is holy, He finds rest among the holy."

It is believed that the girl Mary remained in the temple until her fourteenth year. What did Mary do during those tender years? What occupied her heart, her head and her hands? We know there was a set schedule of balanced prayer and labor followed by these maidens in the temple.

A great deal of time was devoted to prayer — alone and with others. There were three set times for prayer: morning prayer at sunrise; afternoon prayer about three o'clock; evening prayer at sunset.

In between the praises of God Mary worked at weaving and working with wool. In addition she and the other girls took care of the sick who came to them, helped to keep the sacred precincts clean, and devoted much time to the poor.

In such an atmosphere, hidden from the world, barred from the blazing sun of public gaze, Mary grew in virtue and grace. Always "full of grace," the cloistered Maid developed in purity and patience, in charity and humility, and in the spirit of prayer. Her heart sank deep roots into the sources of grace. Her development was hidden.

She was giving herself to God. Would that we could do that in some small measure. She was setting the pattern for those who would serve the Lord through the centuries. May ours be the prayer of the Church on the feast of the Presentation:

"O God, who didst will that Blessed Mary ever-virgin, the dwelling of the Holy Ghost, should today be presented in the temple, grant, we beseech Thee, that, through her intercession, we may merit to be presented in the temple of Thy glory. Through Jesus Christ, our Lord." Amen.

"There was a marriage in Cana of Galilee: and the mother of Jesus was there." St. John, 2:2.

King Edward VII of England was one day driving along a country road when he overtook an old market woman. She was struggling under a load which was more than she could manage.

"You might take part of this in your carriage," she cried to the king, not recognizing who he was.

"Alas, my good woman," replied his majesty, "I am very sorry, but I am not going the same way. However, let me give you the portrait of my mother."

"A lot of good that will do me," grumbled the woman.

"Take it all the same," urged the king with a smile. Into the palm of the astonished peasant he put a sovereign bearing the picture of Queen Victoria, his mother. A sovereign was worth a couple dollars in our money. The woman did not realize the value of a picture of the king's mother. That picture was on a coin and the coin was valuable.

In a somewhat similar way we can see the sons and daughters of the King of heaven traveling along the highway of life and meeting with difficulties. We can see the heavenly King offering them a picture of His Mother, a portrait that will be of more help to the struggling wayfarer on the road of life than any coin could possibly be, no matter what its value.

On November 27 we celebrate the feast of the Miraculous Medal of Mary Immaculate. Here is the story: In 1806 there was born in France a child who later entered a religious community, the Daughters of Charity. Her name was Sister Catherine Laboure. Her prayer that some day she might see the Blessed Virgin was answered for the first time on July 18, 1830. Mary told Sister Catherine that she was to receive a special mission for the greater glory of God, that the work would bring much suffering, but would also bring many graces.

Our Blessed Lady appeared to Sister Catherine a second time on November 27 of the same year. Mary was beautifully robed, standing on a globe about half of which was visible. In her hands Mary held another globe representing the world, which she seemed to press to her heart. Suddenly this globe disappeared, and on our Blessed Mother's fingers were a number of rings set with precious gems. From these gems came rays of light shining on all sides and completely surrounding Our Lady. As the young novice gazed in awe, Mary explained:

"The globe which you see represents the world and every single person."

About our Blessed Mother was a frame on which appeared in letters of gold this prayer:

"O Mary, conceived without sin, pray for us who have recourse to thee."

Then the novice heard a voice:

"Have a medal made according to this model; all who wear it will receive great graces, especially if they wear it around the neck. Graces will be abundant for those who have confidence."

Then the picture seemed to turn around and on the reverse side Sister Catherine saw the letter M surrounded by a cross with a line at the base Underneath the letter M were the hearts of Jesus and Mary, the first en-circled by a crown of thorns and the other pierced with a sword.

In the third and final appearance of Our Lady which took place toward the end of the same year, Mary again made known her wish to have a medal made according to the design given. The part of Sister Catherine in these miraculous appearances remained hidden until her death forty-six years later. Nevertheless, the medal was made according to Our Lady's instruction. It was widely circulated, and within a short time was worn by millions. Through this medal countless favors both of body and soul have been granted. Because of these many blessings the medal soon received, by popular agreement, the name that it commonly bears today, THE MIRAC-ULOUS MEDAL.

On May 28, 1933, Pope Pius XII declared Sister Catherine Blessed Catherine Laboure. This same pontiff also declared:

"The whole world has been filled with miracles due to the holy medal which with reason has been styled miraculous."

Usually this medal is worn suspended from the neck. It may be attached to the neck of a garment. With the wearing should go the prayer: "O Mary, conceived without sin, pray for us who have recourse to thee."

This medal is remarkable for several reasons. Emphasizing the Immaculate Conception, it summarizes the main teachings of the Catholic faith—the fall, the promised Redeemer, the Virgin-Mother, the incarnation, the redemption.

Let's look at the medal a moment. The M represents Mary—Mother and Mediatrix. The cross reminds us of the limitless love of the Son of God. The two hearts of Jesus and Mary tell us of the inseparable love of Mother and Son. The rays of the medal represent the graces that come to us through Mary. The stars represent the twelve Apostles, the men who were to bring the knowledge of Christ to the world, and they remind us of the Queen of the Apostles.

When people hear of the wonders that come to those who wear this medal with faith and devotion, they want to secure one and wear one. The Miraculous Medal offers us a reminder of the principal points of our faith. It brings out also what is sometimes called the fifth mark of the true Church, namely, devotion to the Blessed Virgin Mother of God.

You might make the feast of the Miraculous Medal the occasion to find out more about it, to secure a medal for yourself and your loved ones, and to begin—or to continue with renewed fervor—the wearing of this mani-festly privileged picture of the Mother of our King. Amen.

IMMACULATE CONCEPTION—December 8

"I will put enmities between thee and the woman, and thy seed and her seed: she will crush thy head, and thou shalt lie in wait for her heel." Genesis, 3:15.

In the early years of the seventeenth century the armies of Sweden threatened to overrun Austria. They won victory after victory. The Austrian Emperor, Ferdinand III, was desperate. In 1629 he decided to make a public appeal for the protection of the Blessed Virgin, toward whom he had a tender devotion.

He ordered the building of a giant column in the city square of Vienna. It was decorated with numerous emblems, all representing some phase of the Immaculate Conception. At each of the four corners of the foundation he directed that angels in armor be placed, treading the dragon under their feet, showing how our Spotless Mother won the victory over original sin and all sin. On the summit of the column stood a statue of the Mother of God, her foot on the head of the satanic serpent. At the base of the imposing pillar were carved the words:

"TO THE MOST HIGH AND GOOD GOD, LORD OF HEAVEN AND EARTH, FROM WHOM KINGS HOLD THEIR THRONES.

"TO THE VIRGIN MOTHER OF GOD, CONCEIVED WITHOUT STAIN OF ORIGINAL SIN, BY WHOM PRINCES COMMAND, WHO HAS THIS DAY BEEN CHOSEN BY PARTICULAR DEVOTION AS PATRONESS OF AUSTRIA, THE EMPEROR FERDINAND III ENTRUSTS AND CONSECRATES ALL HIS POSSESSIONS, HIS PERSON, HIS CHILDREN, HIS PEOPLE, HIS ARMIES, HIS DOMAINS; AND IN PERPETUAL MEMORY OF THIS, HIS DEVOTION, HE HAS ERECTED THIS STATUE."

Never in the history of the land was there a more solemn celebration than that which marked the dedication of this splendid shaft. It gave triumphant testimony to their love of the Immaculate Conception of Mary.

The devout emperor marched in the procession, attended by his son Ferdinand IV, who was king of Bohemia and Hungary, by his daughter Marianna, who was queen of Spain, by representatives of many countries. by all the nobility, by religious communities and by the secular clergy. An immense crowd followed as the pious parade made its way to the foot of the column. There the emperor repeated aloud and with all the fervor of his soul the words inscribed in stone, the words inscribed in their hearts, the words consecrating and dedicating himself and his kingdom and his people to the Immaculate Mother of God.

How pleasing this dedication was to Mary is seen in the sudden and striking assistance she sent to those who honored her Immaculate Conception. Motherlike she hurried to help. A few days after this magnificent demonstration the emperor met the enemy at Eger, close to the invaders' camp. With one blow he stopped the oncoming Swedes and forced them to sign a complete and lasting treaty of peace. His empire was saved.

Austria, or any other nation, never had more invaders than America has today. True, we do have friends. But those who plot our downfall are so great and numerous, so secret and satanic, that every true American must awaken to threatening enemies from within and without. There is no cause for hysteria, but there is need to realize that certain forces, foreign to the spirit of America, are working to wreck our glorious nation.

There is, for instance, a godless government called the Soviet, which openly admits its purpose to envelop us within its Iron Curtain. Agents of that Red regime are working in all classes and professions and in many departments of our government, to bring about the overthrow of all that we Americans hold sacred.

How long it takes some people to wake up! For decades the Catholic Church has been warning the world about Atheistic Communism. Only when war is waged in helpless Korea do some eyes and minds open.

Knowingly and unknowingly thousands of so-called Americans are working against our government. Our schools are honeycombed with teachers who are against God, the very foundation of our nation.

Another group who profess to believe in God are openly and secretly working against God's Church, the Catholic Church, the most patriotic and powerful force for true Americanism in the land. In college classrooms, in Protestant pulpits, in secret societies, in telephone, back-fence, and bridge-club gossip there is ceaseless sniping at the beliefs and practices of a spiritual organization which stands and fights for every basic principle of the United States.

In this army invading America we see the greedy capitalist and the merciless money-changer who give ground to the charge of capitalist cruelty. Thank God, not all managers and owners are lined up with them.

The invaders include racketeers and fomenters of violence, race hatred and bigotry, printers and peddlers of impure literature, producers and patrons of immoral movies, sellers and buyers of birth control misinformation.

In that army we see Blanshards and Oxnams, so-called converted Catholics and Witnesses of Jehovah, all tearing away at the nation's foundations.

Who can stop such invaders? Who can save our soil from such traitors?

All the policemen in the world, including our FBI and our army cannot repulse such attackers.

Like King Ferdinand and the people of Austria, we Americans will appeal to one who has been victorious before, one who has won the greatest victory of all time, the victory over sin. On December 8 we publicly and lovingly dedicate ourselves again to the Immaculate Virgin and Mother. Ask her help in halting the enemies of the country which chose her as patroness under the title of the Immaculate Conception. May Mary Immaculate, the victorious Virgin, win another victory for us. Amen.

TRANSLATION OF THE HOLY HOUSE OF LORETO—Dec. 10

"And he went down with them and came to Nazareth, and was subject to them." St. Luke, 2:51.

The battle of Lepanto was a turning point of history. It was a victory won by Christians over pagans. In the year 1571 the Turks made themselves masters of the Island of Cyprus. They were about to attack Venice with an army so powerful that it seemed they could conquer the entire world.

Pope Pius V, King Philip II of Spain, and the citizens of Venice joined their forces, which were pitifully few in comparison with the attackers. The followers of Christ begged Our Lady of Loreto to help them. Their commander-in-chief, Don Juan of Austria, made a vow that he would go on a pilgrimage to the famous shrine of Our Lady of Loreto. The Christians won a decisive victory on October 7, 1571. The Turks lost over 40,000 men and a large amount of equipment. As soon as he could straighten out his affairs, Don Juan set out in the depths of winter to accomplish his vow. It was on this occasion that Pope Pius V established the solemn feast of the Rosary which was afterwards fixed by Gregory XIII.

Who is this Lady of Loreto, and what was the shrine by that name? On December 10 we keep the feast with the title THE TRANSLATION OF THE HOLY HOUSE OF LORETO. Loreto is a small town just a few miles south of Ancona, Italy, near the sea. It boasts a huge basilica or church crowned by a tremendous dome. In this church is enshrined a little house only 31 feet by 13 feet. At one end is an altar beneath a statue of the Virgin Mother and her Divine Child. On the little house is an inscription in Latin: "Here the Word was made flesh."

In other words, that tiny house is honored as the very same cottage at Nazareth in which the Son of God became incarnate, and in which the Holy Family lived. Another, longer inscription explains more:

"Christian pilgrim, you have before your eyes the Holy House of Loreto, venerable throughout the world on account of the divine mysteries accomplished in it and the glorious miracles herein wrought. It is here that most Holy Mary, Mother of God, was born; here that she was saluted by the angel, here that the eternal Word of God was made flesh. Angels conveyed this house from Palestine to the town of Tersato in Illyria in the year of salvation 1291. Three years later it was carried again by the ministry of angels and placed in a wood near this hill, in the vicinity of Recanati, in the march of Ancona; where having changed its station thrice in the course of a year, at length, by the will of God, it took up its permanent position on this spot three hundred years ago (which is now over six hundred years). Ever since that time, both the extraordinary nature of the event having called forth the admiring wonder of the neighboring people and the fame of the miracles wrought in this sanctuary having spread far and wide, this holy house, whose walls do not rest on any foundation and yet remain solid and uninjured after so many centuries, has been held in reverence by all nations."

In other words, the translation of the Holy House of Loreto really means the carrying by angels from Palestine to Italy of the very house in which Mary was born, where Jesus was conceived, where Jesus, Mary and Joseph lived. This seems to be an impossible legend. Yet, there are many reasons to back it up, four of which we might mention:

1. The repeated approval of this tradition by at least 47 popes inclines us to believe it, as does the fact that many holy men like St. Charles Borromeo, St. Francis de Sales, St. Ignatius of Loyola and others, have paid their respects at this shrine.

2. For centuries Loreto has been the scene of numerous, miraculous cures and wonderful happenings. Even a skeptic like Montaigne professed his **belief in the reality of these wonders.**

3. The stone of the original walls and the mortar are not known in the neighborhood of Loreto, but they are identical with materials common in Nazareth.

4. The Holy House, as it is called, does not rest and has never rested on any solid foundation, something miraculous in itself.

Nevertheless, there are arguments against this legend. Certain historical and scientific testimony indicate that this could not be the home of the Holy Family. Much has been written for and against.

But one fact remains uncontested—Our Lady of Loreto has obtained countless miracles from God. Of that we are sure. Hence, whether it is the actual home of Jesus, Mary and Joseph or not, it is a place of spiritual power.

Furthermore, anyone who has ever thought about the homelife of the Holy Family has no doubt pictured in his mind that holy home, and has expressed the desire to visit it, or that the home itself could be in the place where the Christian is. In that sense I think it is appropriate and in line with God's plan that this Holy House of Nazareth be present not only in Loreto in Italy, but that it be present in every village, every town, and every city in the world.

To me that points up one of the reasons for the importance of this feast. Holy homes are the greatest need in the world today. Devotion to the Holy House at Loreto will promote holy homes. There is absolutely nothing that will build happy, holy homes more effectively than devotion to the home life of the Holy Family. Loreto will keep us constantly in mind of those Holy Three.

May this coming feast make us think of that Holy House. May this feast bring the Holy House into the hearts of every one of us. May the angels carry into our hearts every detail of the blessed abode of Jesus, Mary and Joseph. Amen.

OUR LADY OF GUADALUPE—December 12

"Who is she that cometh forth as the morning rising, fair as the moon, bright as the sun?" Canticles, 6:9.

It was early morning, Saturday, December 9, 1531. An old Indian was picking his way along a rocky path through the hills that led to Mexico City. He was one of the many converted by the zealous missionaries of the time. He was on his way to Mass and instruction. His name was Juan Diego.

Suddenly he heard sweet music, so sweet that it seemed of another world. As he looked and listened he beheld a beautiful woman. In the center of a dazzling light in the nearby rocks stood the Blessed Virgin. She smiled sweetly and kindly upon him as the Indian stood there speechless.

"Juan, my son," she directed, "go to Bishop Zumarraga, a Franciscan. Tell him that the Virgin Mary desires a church erected on this spot. Hasten now."

The vision vanished as quickly as it had come. Juan stumbled on his way still stunned by the sight of the beauteous Lady. A few hours later he related his story to Bishop Zumarraga, the first bishop of Mexico City, a spiritual leader who loved his people. Patiently the prelate heard the story. But his mind was doubtful, and when Diego had finished his tale, the bishop placed a kindly hand on his shoulder and said:

"Yes, yes, Juan. It is interesting, this story of yours. We shall think it over."

But the next day, Sunday, the bishop again found Juan waiting to tell him of a second appearance. The bishop asked him many questions, trying to find mistakes in his story. He sat back and told Diego:

"Juan, I would like to believe you, but I do not know. I must have some sign, some token from the Blessed Virgin that you are telling the truth."

Juan promised to ask the Blessed Mother for some sign. On his way home Mary appeared again and assured him of a sign. However, Juan stopped to visit a seriously sick uncle, for whom he went to seek a priest.

As he came to the hill where Mary had appeared to him he remembered that he was supposed to come back on Monday. Since he was afraid of her reproaches, he took a different route. But our Blessed Mother appeared to him nevertheless with the question:

"What road is this thou hast taken, my son?"

"My child," Juan answered using this endearing name, "a servant of yours, my uncle, is dangerously sick of a grave and mortal malady."

He then told her that he was on his way to get a priest, that he would come tomorrow without fail. Mary assured him that his uncle's illness had passed and that he would not die of it. Then Mary told him to go over to the spot on the mountain where she had first appeared to him and gather some roses. It was not the time for flowers of any kind. It was winter.

100

Besides, roses never grew in that region. Nevertheless Juan obeyed and he did find beautiful roses. He gathered them ino his cloak and hurried to the bishop who was waiting with a group of officials of church and government. As Juan came into the room the bishop greeted him with these fatherly words:

"Well, my son, what news have you?"

"My father, I have the sign you asked," answered Juan.

"A sign," repeated the bishop, leaning forward, "where is it?"

"Here in my cloak," said Juan and then he told how Mary had directed him to gather roses. He faltered and went on:

"With her own hands Our Lady arranged the flowers; then she told me to cover them with my cloak and bring them to you untouched and unseen. Here, my father, is the sign you asked—the roses of Guadalupe."

Juan opened his cloak. The glorious, fragrant roses fell at the feet of the bishop. No sooner did the prelate and the people with him notice the roses than they noticed something else on the Indian's cloak. There on the coarse cloth was painted a picture, a life-size picture of the Blessed Virgin just as Juan had seen her and described her. That was sign sufficient for the bishop.

A small chapel was built on the spot where Mary had appeared to this poor, simple Indian, a chapel that was repeatedly replaced with a larger and larger building until finally today there is a huge basilica, the center, the heart of a devotion to Our Lady of Guadalupe that has not only swept Mexico but has influenced the entire world.

The picture was closely guarded, but immediately pilgrimages, processions and groups from all over the countryside began to make their way to this shrine. Countless miracles were obtained. Countless conversions were effected.

Pope Benedict XIV decreed that Our Lady of Guadalupe should be Mexico's national patron, and today she is recognized as the Queen of the America's. Our present Pope Pius XII, as Cardinal Pacelli in 1933 crowned the picture painted by Cabrera which had been given to Pope Benedict XIV.

We Americans who have this shrine of Our Mother in our midst, as it were, here upon the American continent, might well repeat the prayer of the Most Rev. John J. Cantwell composed for the coronation of Our Lady of Guadalupe in Los Angeles:

"Immaculate Virgin of Guadalupe, heavenly missionary of the New World, thy sweet charm holds the hearts of thy people. Blessed Mother of God, from thy sanctuary of Tepeyac, monument of the love of all America for you, that hast been for centuries the mother and teacher of our people; be also our refuge, our defense, and unto us a pillar of strength. O Most Immaculate Mary, protect and save our republic, our superiors and rulers and all the people of our continent."

Many Americans, non-Catholic as well as Catholic, have visited her shrine. The Mexicans in the United States have brought with them from Old Mexico this flaming love for Our Lady of Guadalupe. But she belongs to all of us, especially to all Americans. On her feast tell Mary that you want to belong to her. Amen.

QUEEN OF THE ORDER OF FRIARS MINOR (Franciscans)
December 15

"In all these I sought rest, and I shall abide in the inheritance of the Lord."
Ecclesiasticus, 24:11.

Tongues in the town of Siena were wagging. One of the village lads was going frequently for solitary walks in the woods. One day his aunt asked him where he was going. Simply he answered:

"I am calling on my sweetheart."

This explanation seemed stranger than his actions, for he had never shown any interest in the young ladies of the town. Who could this sweetheart be? His sister decided to trail him. Far into the forest her brother hurried, so fast that she almost lost track of him. Suddenly in a dense thicket she came upon her brother kneeling hat in hand before a small statue of the Blessed Virgin. About the image he had woven a little covering of branches and rocks. So that was the sweetheart of her brother, who was later to become the saintly and eloquent Bernardine of Siena.

Mary always remained St. Bernardine's sweetheart. She has been the sweetheart of every true Franciscan.

Orphaned at seven, Bernardine was entrusted to a virtuous aunt who filled his heart with a tender devotion to his Blessed Mother. Before he was ten he fasted every Saturday in honor of Mary. He had been born and baptized on Mary's birthday, September 8, 1380. He chose that day for the principal actions of his life: on September 8 he took the holy habit of St. Francis; on that day he made his vows; on that same date he was ordained a priest and preached his first sermon, yes, you guessed it, a sermon on his heavenly Queen. A natural impediment of speech, a weak and hoarse voice were remedied by beseeching his glorious patroness, God's Mother.

With his growing fame as a preacher, Bernardine's love for Our Lady waxed warm and eloquent. Repeatedly he reminded his audiences of her virtues and privileges. As Commissary General of the Franciscan Order he warmly approved and fostered devotion to the Seven Joys, favorite Marian prayer of the seraphic family. Through his efforts the name of Jesus was added to the Angel's salutation, the first half of the Hail Mary. His death during Mary's month, May 20, 1444, put the seal on his love for her.

The beloved of this famous Franciscan has been the beloved of every other worthy member of the Franciscan family. Filial love for her marks every one who ever wore worthily the brown habit and the white cord. The sons and daughters of St. Francis come by this love honestly, as if by heredity. The Seraphic Saint had a flaming love for Mary.

From his youth Francis yearned to honor and imitate "the Mother all-loving," "the Mistress of the world." He praised and imitated her poverty. Once while sitting at dinner with several friars, someone remarked how poor our Blessed Mother was on Christmas day. So strongly was Francis affected that he left the table, sat on the bare floor, and finished his frugal fare in tears.

He consecrated himself and his followers to the Mother of God, Mother of the poor. She had watched by the cradle at Bethlehem; he begged her to watch by the poor cradle of his Order, the Portiuncula. Thither he led new members to introduce them as it were to their Mother. Thither he hurried in doubts and difficulties. Thither he hastened on his return from mission tours. Thither, as to the fire-place, the center of things seraphic, he found his way for strength and grace and consolation.

Not content with the prayers of the liturgy, he made up praises of his own, tender aspirations to his Mother. Most charming of these love poems is "THE SALUTATION OF THE BLESSED VIRGIN," written and often repeated by our saint:

"Hail, holy Lady, most holy queen,
"Mother of God, Mary!
"Who art ever Virgin,
"Chosen from heaven by the most holy Father!
"Whom He has consecrated with the most beloved Son,
"And the Spirit, the Paraclete!
"In whom was and is all the fulness of grace and all good.
"Hail thou His palace!
"Hail thou His tabernacle!
"Hail thou His house!
"Hail thou His garment!
"Hail thou His handmaid!
"Hail thou His mother!"

All Franciscans caught this flame. To mention but a few: St. Bonaventure and the Angelus; St. Bernardine and the prayer, "We fly to thy patronage, O holy Mother of God"; St. Anthony and his "Sermon on the Praises of Mary"; Scotus and the Immaculate Conception; the Seven Joys; the Espousals; the concluding words of the Hail Mary "now and at the hour of our death."

This and more led Pope Pius X to declare to the world:

"We, from the fullness of our Apostolic power and as a new token of our special good will towards the sons of St. Francis, grant and command.... that in the Litany of Loreto...the Seraphic Order add, 'QUEEN OF THE FRIARS MINOR, PRAY FOR US.'

"We declare that by means of this invocation the special protection of the Immaculate Virgin is implored: First, for the members of the three-fold branch of the Franciscan Order collectively and individually, and for their Ministers General; secondly, for the nuns who follow the Rule of St. Clare ...; thirdly, for the members of the Third Order of either sex whether they live in community or in the world ..."

Pope Pius XII set the Feast on December 15, and granted a special Mass.

Queen and Sweetheart—may Mary ever be that to every Franciscan. Amen.

EXPECTATION OF OUR LADY—December 18

"She shall bring forth a son, and thou shalt call his name Jesus; for he shall save his people from their sins." St. Matthew, 1:21.

Several years ago a touching story came out of Joplin, Missouri. Living there at the time was a married woman by the name of Zoe Tucker Peterson. She was thirty-two years old and for twelve years had been bedfast with arthritis. Her husband, a childhood sweetheart, was a laborer. One day she announced to him that she was going to have a baby. She was most happy and cheerful about it, as we can see from her following words:

"All my adult life I have had a rendezvous with death. Now I have a rendezvous with life. My baby will live and will be loved. The doctors have told me that I have a 50-50 chance. I am happy because never before have I had that much of a chance."

On her thirty-second birthday this woman was to exchange her life for the life of another. Happy and cheerfully expectant, she went to the hospital to await the arrival of her child. Zoe had no fear of death because she had lived so near to it for so many years. She gave birth to a son who weighed four and a half pounds. But—a few hours after the birth of her child the mother passed away, without ever seeing on this earth the tiny son upon whom she had bestowed the greatest gift that anyone can give, the gift of life.

In the heart of this martyr mother we see some of the sentiments that must have been in the heart of the Blessed Virgin as she awaited the birth of her Son, Jesus. During these days before Christmas Mother Church centers many of her thoughts on Mary, and on December 18 we celebrate the feast of the Expectation of Our Lady, no doubt with the idea of directing us to think of the heart and emotions of Mary during that period.

The time of expectation is a trying time, a tender, delicate time, a time when mother must make many sacrifices, when mother must put up with many discomforts. But for Mary it was full of deep thoughts about the Almighty God and the role and part she was playing in the redemption of the world. Like that young mother from Joplin, Missouri, Mary too had deep in her heart a spirit of sacrifice. Courageously she looked forward to the sorrows and trials that would be hers as the Mother of the Redeemer. Happily she waited for God's good time when her Child would be born. There are some sentiments Mary had at this time upon which we would like to center our thoughts as we approach the feast of the Expectation:

1. Before the birth of Christ Mary had shown her spirit of charity by visiting her cousin Elizabeth. Likewise she had shown her spirit of self-denial and of humility. Foremost in her heart was the thought: "I am the Mother of God."

How happy and also how humble that thought must have made her. It must have made her pray with sincerity and deep dependence upon the help of the Almighty. She was exalted above all mankind, she was chosen from all the women of all time to give a human nature to the Son of God. Far from making her proud and haughty, this fact made her profoundly humble.

It made her adore and praise the decree of the Divinity that gave her this wonderful grace. Again and again Mary must have repeated the words of her song: "He that is mighty hath done great things to me." St. Luke, 1:49.

Uppermost in her desires was the wish to imitate the self-abasement of Him whom she carried.

2. She had another thought:

"I am the Mother of the Redeemer, the Mother of Him for whom the world has been praying and longing since the beginning of human history, the Mother of Him who will give Himself for the salvation of mankind. That Redeemer, that Messias, that Promised One I am carrying within me."

Her heart was full of love for the Son who would give Himself to save all.

3. Though Mary realized her great privileges and honors, she kept repeating the touching words:

"Behold the handmaid of the Lord."

In this spirit of subjection to the designs of the Almighty Mary passed this tender time of waiting for the birth of the Redeemer.

4. In these sentiments of Mary's heart during the time of her Expectation we find a model for our emotions with regard to Holy Communion. When we receive our Lord He becomes present within us. Then we too are carrying Christ within us. It is a high and happy honor, that also makes us humbly grateful, as it did Mary.

5. Another thought suggests itself with regard to the Expectation of Our Lady, namely, the attention and kindness of St. Joseph toward Mary during this delicate time. Here St. Joseph is a perfect model for all husbands whose wives are awaiting the moment of delivery. He is a model for our attitude and our consideration toward all who are expecting the arrival of a child.

We emphasize this in a day when expectant mothers are often made the butt of criticism and even ridicule. How trying that must be to an expectant mother. And how utterly pagan and pitiless such criticism is.

Such mothers might look to Mary who for a time was an object of criticism and suspicion. With the help of her devoted spouse she weathered all these storms.

Just as you and I, had we been living in those days before the birth of Jesus, would have done anything to help Our Blessed Mother, to make her days and hours more comfortable, so today, in honor of Mary, we should show other mothers the consideration and helpfulness we might have shown to Mary. If we do it in that spirit, Mary will reward us.

May the feast of the Expectation remind us of these sentiments of Our Lady. Make her your model for your attitude toward all motherhood. Amen.

TOPICAL INDEX